Lectio Divina of the Gospels

for the Liturgical Year 2018-2019

United States Conference of Catholic Bishops

Epigraph quote taken from Guigo II, *The Ladder of Monks and Twelve Meditations*. Trans. Edmund Colledge, O.S.A. and James Walsh, S.J. (Collegeville: Cistercian Publications, Inc., 1981 [Cisterician Studies no. 48]) 68-69.

First Printing, September 2018

ISBN 978-1-60137-605-3

Contents

Reading seeks for the sweetness of a blessed life,
meditation perceives it,
prayer asks for it,
contemplation tastes it.

Reading, as it were, puts food whole into the mouth,
meditation chews it and breaks it up,
prayer extracts its flavor,
contemplation is the sweetness itself
which gladdens and refreshes.

Reading works on the outside,
meditation on the pith,
prayer asks for what we long for,
contemplation gives us delight in the sweetness
which we have found.

— Guigo II, *The Ladder of Monks*, III (12th c.)

What Is *Lectio Divina* and How to Use This Book

Reading – Meditation – Prayer – Contemplation

Lectio divina or "divine reading" is a process of engaging with Christ, the Word of God. Through this sacred exercise, we enter into a closer relationship with the very Word himself, who communicates the love of the Father to us through the Holy Spirit.

Lectio divina has four steps in which we first hear what God has said (reading). We then take it in and reflect on it (meditation). From this our hearts are lifted up (prayer). Finally, after speaking to the Lord in prayer, we rest and listen for his message to us (contemplation).

This is the process of *lectio divina*. It is a conversation with God, grounded in God's own self-revelation to us. This helps us speak to God with a focus on what he has already told us about his relationship with humanity, his plans and desires for us, his promises, his admonitions, and his guidance on how we can live, so as to find true life in abundance in Christ.

Here is a brief description of each of the four steps:

Reading (*Lectio*)

Read the passage slowly and allow it to sink in.

If there is a passage that is particularly striking, and that you want to keep with you, consider committing it to memory, or writing it down to keep with you, so that you can re-read it throughout the day, and let it enter deeper into your spirit.

"Faith comes from what is heard, and what is heard comes through the word of Christ." (Romans 10:17)

"The word of God is living and effective, sharper than any two-edged sword, penetrating even between soul and spirit, joints and marrow, and able to discern reflections and thoughts of the heart."
(Hebrews 4:12)

Meditation (*Meditatio*)

Read the passage again, and when something strikes you, a question arises in you, stop and meditate. Think about what God may be saying through it.

"It is the glory of God to conceal a matter,
and the glory of kings to fathom a matter."
(Proverbs 25:2)

"I will ponder your precepts and consider your paths." (Psalm 119:15)

Prayer (*Oratio*)

Speak to the Lord about what you have read and share what's on your mind and heart—offer and share with the Lord your thanksgiving, petition, concerns, doubts, or simply affirm, back to the Lord, the very word that he has spoken.

"Enter his gates with thanksgiving,
his courts with praise."
(Psalm 100:4)

"Ask and it will be given to you; seek and you will find; knock and the door will be opened to you." (Matthew 7:7)

Contemplation (*Contemplatio*)

This is a quiet time, a time to rest in his presence and wait upon the Lord. It is a time where we allow the Lord to speak directly to our spirit from within us. It requires practice. But this allows us to be attentive to the Lord's voice, and by regular practice, our ability to hear God's voice will grow in daily life and daily situations, as we learn to focus our minds and hearts, our thoughts, our concerns, and our hopes toward him.

"My sheep hear my voice; I know them, and they follow me." (John 10:27)

"Be still and know that I am God!" (Psalm 46:11)

Applying This Process of *Lectio Divina* to the Liturgical Year

This *Lectio Divina of the Gospels for the Liturgical Year* book will take the reader through the Sundays and major feasts and solemnities of the liturgical year. It can be used for individual devotion and can also easily be used to assist in small group reflections in parishes and small faith groups. It offers a structured process for engaging with the Word of God. As the reader or group becomes more comfortable engaging with Scripture, this process can be more closely tailored to suit the path of growth that best fits the reader(s).

First, the *lectio divina* session is started by praying a prayer that is taken from a Mass collect from that liturgical week. Following that prayer, the main scripture passage for reflection is read, which is taken from the gospel reading for that day. This READING can be re-read, a few times, to let it sink in. Next, a set of three questions are offered to help in MEDITATION. These questions can also facilitate talking about the passage in a group setting. The individual then offers his or her personal PRAYER, responding to the Lord. In a group setting, people can speak out their prayers one at a time—this may help deepen the prayer response and further set the group's focus on the Lord.

Next, a structured set of passages and questions are offered that return the reader back to the gospel passage. This invites the reader to contemplate what the Lord is speaking and what it means for their life. It allows the individual or the prayer group to consider specific ways the Lord may be speaking into their life at that very moment. As each person begins to hear a response from the Lord—the Lord's word spoken directly and personally to them—that person can begin let that word flow through their life, by an interior change and a will to do what the Lord is asking of them. Through this step of CONTEMPLATION, we hear God's voice speaking to us, and it propels us to conversion of heart and mind.

After the closing prayer, time is given to choosing how to live out the fruit of your prayer. You know your heart and life best—if it's clear what God is asking of you, in faith, choose some way that you can put that request or teaching from the Lord into action that week. It could be a small act of faith that the Lord is asking, or perhaps, a more serious and important step that he is asking you to take. If there is nothing specific that comes to your mind, consider the question and suggestion offered in the *Living the Word This Week* section. This portion offers guidance on what concrete actions may be taken in our daily lives.

The *Lectio Divina of the Gospels for the Liturgical Year* offers a specific pattern of prayerful reading of God's Word. As you begin on this path, may the Lord's blessing follow you, and fall upon you, throughout the movement of seasons in this new liturgical year, and may your life, in turn, be a blessing upon others.

Lectio Divina of the Gospels

December 2, 2018

Lectio Divina for the First Week of Advent

We begin our prayer:
In the name of the Father, and of the Son, and of the Holy Spirit.
Amen.

Stir up your power, O Lord,
and come to our help with mighty strength,
that what our sins impede
the grace of your mercy may hasten.
Through our Lord Jesus Christ, your Son,
who lives and reigns with you in the unity of the Holy Spirit,
one God, for ever and ever.

(Collect, Thursday of the First Week of Advent)

Reading (*Lectio*)

Read the following Scripture two or three times.
Luke 21:25-28, 34-36

Jesus said to his disciples: "There will be signs in the sun, the moon, and the stars, and on earth nations will be in dismay, perplexed by the roaring of the sea and the waves. People will die of fright in anticipation of what is coming upon the world, for the powers of the heavens will be shaken. And then they will see the Son of Man coming in a cloud with power and great glory. But when these signs begin to happen, stand erect and raise your heads because your redemption is at hand.

"Beware that your hearts do not become drowsy from carousing and drunkenness and the anxieties of daily life, and that day catch you by surprise like a trap. For that day will assault everyone who lives on the face of the earth. Be vigilant at all times and pray that you have the strength to escape the tribulations that are imminent and to stand before the Son of Man."

Meditation (*Meditatio*)

After the reading, take some time to reflect in silence on one or more of the following questions:

- What word or words in this passage caught your attention?
- What in this passage comforted you?
- What in this passage challenged you?

If practicing lectio divina *as a family or in a group, after the reflection time, invite the participants to share their responses.*

Prayer (*Oratio*)

Read the Scripture passage one more time. Bring to the Lord the praise, petition, or thanksgiving that the Word inspires in you.

Contemplation (*Contemplatio*)

Read the Scripture again, followed by this reflection:

What conversion of mind, heart, and life is the Lord asking of me?

People will die of fright in anticipation of what is coming upon the world. What events and situations in the world create fear and concern in my heart? How can I be a force for peace and justice?

Beware that your hearts do not become drowsy from carousing and drunkenness and the anxieties of daily life. What anxieties or circumstances in my daily life make my heart drowsy? How can I wake my heart to love of God and neighbor?

Be vigilant at all times and pray. When am I least attentive to God and neighbor? How can I increase my vigilance in prayer and action?

After a period of silent reflection and/or discussion, all recite the Lord's Prayer and the following:

Closing Prayer:

Your ways, O LORD, make known to me;
teach me your paths,
Guide me in your truth and teach me,
for you are God my savior,
and for you I wait all the day.

Good and upright is the LORD;
thus he shows sinners the way.
He guides the humble to justice,
and teaches the humble his way.

All the paths of the LORD are kindness and constancy
toward those who keep his covenant and his decrees.
The friendship of the LORD is with those who fear him,
and his covenant, for their instruction.

(From Psalm 25)

Living the Word This Week

How can I make my life a gift for others in charity?

Every day this week, pray for some event or need that you see in the headlines.

Thoughts for Today

December 8, 2018

Lectio Divina for the Solemnity of the Immaculate Conception

We begin our prayer:
In the name of the Father, and of the Son, and of the Holy Spirit. Amen.

O God, who by the Immaculate Conception of the Blessed Virgin
prepared a worthy dwelling for your Son,
grant, we pray,
that, as you preserved her from every stain
by virtue of the Death of your Son, which you foresaw,
so, through her intercession,
we, too, may be cleansed and admitted to your presence.
Through our Lord Jesus Christ, your Son,
who lives and reigns with you in the unity of the Holy Spirit,
one God, for ever and ever.

(Collect, Immaculate Conception)

Reading (*Lectio*)

Read the following Scripture two or three times.
Luke 1:26-38

The angel Gabriel was sent from God to a town of Galilee called Nazareth, to a virgin betrothed to a man named Joseph, of the house of David, and the virgin's name was Mary. And coming to her, he said, "Hail, full of grace! The Lord is with you." But she was greatly troubled at what was said and pondered what sort of greeting this might be. Then the angel said to her, "Do not be afraid, Mary, for you have found favor with God. Behold, you will conceive in your womb and bear a son, and you shall name him Jesus. He will be great and will be called Son of the Most High, and the Lord God will give him the throne of David his father, and he will rule over the house of Jacob forever, and of his Kingdom there will be no end." But Mary said to the angel, "How can this be, since I have no relations with a man?" And the angel said to her in reply, "The Holy Spirit will come upon you, and the power of the Most High will overshadow you. Therefore the child to be born will be called holy, the Son of God. And behold, Elizabeth, your relative, has also conceived a son in her old age, and this is the sixth month for her who was called barren; for nothing will be impossible for God." Mary said, "Behold, I am the handmaid of the Lord. May it be done to me according to your word." Then the angel departed from her.

Meditation (*Meditatio*)

After the reading, take some time to reflect in silence on one or more of the following questions:

- What word or words in this passage caught your attention?
- What in this passage comforted you?
- What in this passage challenged you?

If practicing lectio divina *as a family or in a group, after the reflection time, invite the participants to share their responses.*

Prayer (*Oratio*)

Read the Scripture passage one more time. Bring to the Lord the praise, petition, or thanksgiving that the Word inspires in you.

Contemplation (*Contemplatio*)

Read the Scripture again, followed by this reflection:

What conversion of mind, heart, and life is the Lord asking of me?

But she was greatly troubled at what was said and pondered what sort of greeting this might be. What aspects of my life create anxiety or trouble? How can my faith in God help me to address these concerns?

For nothing will be impossible for God. What challenges do I need to bring to God? How can I help others bear their burdens?

Behold, I am the handmaid of the Lord. May it be done to me according to your word. To what is God calling me? How can I be more receptive to God's call?

After a period of silent reflection and/or discussion, all recite the Lord's Prayer and the following:

Closing Prayer:

Sing to the LORD a new song,
for he has done wondrous deeds;
His right hand has won victory for him,
his holy arm.

The LORD has made his salvation known:
in the sight of the nations he has revealed his justice.
He has remembered his kindness and his faithfulness
toward the house of Israel.

All the ends of the earth have seen
the salvation by our God.
Sing joyfully to the LORD, all you lands;
break into song; sing praise.

(From Psalm 98)

Living the Word This Week

How can I make my life a gift for others in charity?

Pray for young people who are discerning the vocation to which God is calling them.

Thoughts for Today

December 9, 2018

Lectio Divina for the Second Week of Advent

We begin our prayer:
In the name of the Father, and of the Son, and of the Holy Spirit.
Amen.

Stir up our hearts, O Lord,
to make ready the paths
of your Only Begotten Son,
that through his coming,
we may be found worthy to serve you
with minds made pure.
Through our Lord Jesus Christ, your Son,
who lives and reigns with you in the unity of the Holy Spirit,
one God, for ever and ever.

(Collect, Thursday of the Second Week of Advent)

Reading (*Lectio*)

Read the following Scripture two or three times.
Luke 3:1-6

In the fifteenth year of the reign of Tiberius Caesar, when Pontius Pilate was governor of Judea, and Herod was tetrarch of Galilee, and his brother Philip tetrarch of the region of Ituraea and Trachonitis, and Lysanias was tetrarch of Abilene, during the high priesthood of Annas and Caiaphas, the word of God came to John the son of Zechariah in the desert. John went throughout the whole region of the Jordan, proclaiming a baptism of repentance for the forgiveness of sins, as it is written in the book of the words of the prophet Isaiah:

A voice of one crying out in the desert:
"Prepare the way of the Lord,
make straight his paths.
Every valley shall be filled
and every mountain and hill shall be made low.
The winding roads shall be made straight,
and the rough ways made smooth,
and all flesh shall see the salvation of God."

Meditation (*Meditatio*)

After the reading, take some time to reflect in silence on one or more of the following questions:

- What word or words in this passage caught your attention?
- What in this passage comforted you?
- What in this passage challenged you?

If practicing lectio divina *as a family or in a group, after the reflection time, invite the participants to share their responses.*

Prayer (*Oratio*)

Read the Scripture passage one more time. Bring to the Lord the praise, petition, or thanksgiving that the Word inspires in you.

Contemplation (*Contemplatio*)

Read the Scripture again, followed by this reflection:

What conversion of mind, heart, and life is the Lord asking of me?

The word of God came to John the son of Zechariah in the desert. Where am I most attentive to the voice of God? What distracts me from the Word of God?

Proclaiming a baptism of repentance for the forgiveness of sins. What message is God asking me to share through my words and actions? From what sins do I need to repent?

The winding roads shall be made straight, and the rough ways made smooth. What people, places, or things entice me to veer away from God's path? How can I help ease the path of others?

After a period of silent reflection and/or discussion, all recite the Lord's Prayer and the following:

Closing Prayer:

When the LORD brought back the captives of Zion,
  we were like men dreaming.
Then our mouth was filled with laughter,
  and our tongue with rejoicing.

Then they said among the nations,
  "The LORD has done great things for them."
The LORD has done great things for us;
  we are glad indeed.

Restore our fortunes, O LORD,
  like the torrents in the southern desert.
Those who sow in tears
  shall reap rejoicing.

Although they go forth weeping,
  carrying the seed to be sown,
They shall come back rejoicing,
  carrying their sheaves.

(From Psalm 126)

Living the Word This Week

How can I make my life a gift for others in charity?

Spend time diligently examining your conscience and then receive the Sacrament of Penance.

Thoughts for Today

December 16, 2018

Lectio Divina for the Third Week of Advent

We begin our prayer:
In the name of the Father, and of the Son, and of the Holy Spirit. Amen.

Incline a merciful ear to our cry, we pray, O Lord,
and, casting light on the darkness of our hearts,
visit us with the grace of your Son.
Who lives and reigns with you in the unity of the Holy Spirit,
one God, for ever and ever.

(Collect, Monday of the Third Week of Advent)

Reading (*Lectio*)

Read the following Scripture two or three times.
Luke 3:10-18

The crowds asked John the Baptist, "What should we do?" He said to them in reply, "Whoever has two cloaks should share with the person who has none. And whoever has food should do likewise." Even tax collectors came to be baptized and they said to him, "Teacher, what should we do?" He answered them, "Stop collecting more than what is prescribed." Soldiers also asked him, "And what is it that we should do?" He told them, "Do not practice extortion, do not falsely accuse anyone, and be satisfied with your wages."

Now the people were filled with expectation, and all were asking in their hearts whether John might be the Christ. John answered them all, saying, "I am baptizing you with water, but one mightier than I is coming. I am not worthy to loosen the thongs of his sandals. He will baptize you with the Holy Spirit and fire. His winnowing fan is in his hand to clear his threshing floor and to gather the wheat into his barn, but the chaff he will burn with unquenchable fire." Exhorting them in many other ways, he preached good news to the people.

Meditation (*Meditatio*)

After the reading, take some time to reflect in silence on one or more of the following questions:

- What word or words in this passage caught your attention?
- What in this passage comforted you?
- What in this passage challenged you?

If practicing lectio divina *as a family or in a group, after the reflection time, invite the participants to share their responses.*

Prayer (*Oratio*)

Read the Scripture passage one more time. Bring to the Lord the praise, petition, or thanksgiving that the Word inspires in you.

Contemplation (*Contemplatio*)

Read the Scripture again, followed by this reflection:

What conversion of mind, heart, and life is the Lord asking of me?

The crowds asked John the Baptist, "What should we do?" How can I discern God's will for me? How does my faith influence the decisions in my daily life?

Whoever has two cloaks should share with the person who has none. And whoever has food should do likewise. How can I be more generous with my time, talent, and treasure? How can I encounter and accompany those who are in need?

Exhorting them in many other ways, he preached good news to the people. Through what channels do I hear the good news? How can I share the good news in word and action?

After a period of silent reflection and/or discussion, all recite the Lord's Prayer and the following:

Closing Prayer:

God indeed is my savior;
  I am confident and unafraid.
My strength and my courage is the LORD,
  and he has been my savior.
With joy you will draw water
  at the fountain of salvation.

Give thanks to the LORD, acclaim his name;
  among the nations make known his deeds,
  proclaim how exalted is his name.

Sing praise to the LORD for his glorious achievement;
  let this be known throughout all the earth.
Shout with exultation, O city of Zion,
  for great in your midst
  is the Holy One of Israel!

(From Isaiah 12)

Living the Word This Week

How can I make my life a gift for others in charity?

Donate food, clothing, or money to a local food pantry, homeless shelter, or other agency that aids those in need.

Thoughts for Today

December 23, 2018

Lectio Divina for the Fourth Week of Advent

We begin our prayer:
In the name of the Father, and of the Son, and of the Holy Spirit. Amen.

Almighty ever-living God,
as we see how the Nativity of your Son
according to the flesh draws near,
we pray that to us, your unworthy servants,
mercy may flow from your Word,
who chose to become flesh of the Virgin Mary
and establish among us his dwelling,
Jesus Christ our Lord.
Who lives and reigns with you in the unity of the Holy Spirit,
one God, for ever and ever.

(Collect, December 23)

Reading (*Lectio*)

Read the following Scripture two or three times.
Luke 1:39-45

Mary set out and traveled to the hill country in haste to a town of Judah, where she entered the house of Zechariah and greeted Elizabeth. When Elizabeth heard Mary's greeting, the infant leaped in her womb, and Elizabeth, filled with the Holy Spirit, cried out in a loud voice and said, "Blessed are you among women, and blessed is the fruit of your womb. And how does this happen to me, that the mother of my Lord should come to me? For at the moment the sound of your greeting reached my ears, the infant in my womb leaped for joy. Blessed are you who believed that what was spoken to you by the Lord would be fulfilled."

Meditation (*Meditatio*)

After the reading, take some time to reflect in silence on one or more of the following questions:

- What word or words in this passage caught your attention?
- What in this passage comforted you?
- What in this passage challenged you?

If practicing lectio divina *as a family or in a group, after the reflection time, invite the participants to share their responses.*

Prayer (*Oratio*)

Read the Scripture passage one more time. Bring to the Lord the praise, petition, or thanksgiving that the Word inspires in you.

Contemplation (*Contemplatio*)

Read the Scripture again, followed by this reflection:

What conversion of mind, heart, and life is the Lord asking of me?

And how does this happen to me, that the mother of my Lord should come to me? When have I been surprised by the experience of the presence and comfort of the Lord? How do I carry Christ to others?

For at the moment the sound of your greeting reached my ears, the infant in my womb leaped for joy. When does my heart leap for joy? How can I bring joy to those who are in pain and sorrow?

Blessed are you who believed that what was spoken to you by the Lord would be fulfilled. How can I grow in trusting God? How is God's word being fulfilled in my life?

After a period of silent reflection and/or discussion, all recite the Lord's Prayer and the following:

Closing Prayer:

O shepherd of Israel, hearken,
    from your throne upon the cherubim, shine forth.
Rouse your power,
    and come to save us.

Once again, O LORD of hosts,
    look down from heaven, and see;
take care of this vine,
    and protect what your right hand has planted
    the son of man whom you yourself made strong.

May your help be with the man of your right hand,
    with the son of man whom you yourself made strong.
Then we will no more withdraw from you;
    give us new life, and we will call upon your name.

(From Psalm 80)

Living the Word This Week

How can I make my life a gift for others in charity?

Learn more about your parish's outreach to the sick and homebound and their caregivers. Look for a way that you can assist.

Thoughts for Today

Tuesday, December 25, 2019

Lectio Divina for the Solemnity of Christmas

We begin our prayer:
In the name of the Father, and of the Son, and of the Holy Spirit.
Amen.

O God, who wonderfully created the dignity of human nature
and still more wonderfully restored it,
grant, we pray,
that we may share in the divinity of Christ,
who humbled himself to share in our humanity.
Who lives and reigns with you in the unity of the Holy Spirit,
one God, for ever and ever.

(Collect, Christmas, Mass During the Day)

Reading (*Lectio*)

Read the following Scripture two or three times.
John 1:1-5, 9-14

In the beginning was the Word,
    and the Word was with God,
    and the Word was God.
He was in the beginning with God.
All things came to be through him,
    and without him nothing came to be.
What came to be through him was life,
    and this life was the light of the human race;
the light shines in the darkness,
    and the darkness has not overcome it.

The true light, which enlightens everyone, was coming into the world.

He was in the world,
    and the world came to be through him,
    but the world did not know him.
He came to what was his own,
    but his own people did not accept him.

But to those who did accept him he gave power to become children of God, to those who believe in his name, who were born not by natural generation nor by human choice nor by a man's decision but of God.

And the Word became flesh
    and made his dwelling among us,
    and we saw his glory,
    the glory as of the Father's only Son,
    full of grace and truth.

Meditation (*Meditatio*)

After the reading, take some time to reflect in silence on one or more of the following questions:

- What word or words in this passage caught your attention?
- What in this passage comforted you?
- What in this passage challenged you?

If practicing lectio divina *as a family or in a group, after the reflection time, invite the participants to share their responses.*

Prayer (*Oratio*)

Read the Scripture passage one more time. Bring to the Lord the praise, petition, or thanksgiving that the Word inspires in you.

Contemplation (*Contemplatio*)

Read the Scripture again, followed by this reflection:

What conversion of mind, heart, and life is the Lord asking of me?

The true light, which enlightens everyone, was coming into the world. How can I learn more about my faith? How can my values and beliefs bring light to the dark parts of my life and the world?

He came to what was his own, / but his own people did not accept him. Where do I feel as though I am not accepted? Who do I fail to accept as a brother or sister in Christ?

And the Word became flesh / and made his dwelling among us. Where do I feel God's presence most profoundly? How can I make myself a dwelling place for God?

After a period of silent reflection and/or discussion, all recite the Lord's Prayer and the following:

Closing Prayer:

Sing to the LORD a new song,
  for he has done wondrous deeds;
his right hand has won victory for him,
  his holy arm.

The LORD has made his salvation known:
  in the sight of the nations he has revealed his justice.
He has remembered his kindness and his faithfulness
  toward the house of Israel.

All the ends of the earth have seen
  the salvation by our God.
Sing joyfully to the LORD, all you lands;
  break into song; sing praise.

Sing praise to the LORD with the harp,
  with the harp and melodious song.

With trumpets and the sound of the horn
sing joyfully before the King, the LORD.

(From Psalm 98)

Living the Word This Week

How can I make my life a gift for others in charity?

In this holiday season, visit a friend or family member who you have not seen in a while or open your home to someone who is alone.

Thoughts for Today

December 30, 2018

Lectio Divina for the Feast of the Holy Family of Jesus, Mary, and Joseph

We begin our prayer:
In the name of the Father, and of the Son, and of the Holy Spirit.
Amen.

O God, who were pleased to give us
the shining example of the Holy Family,
graciously grant that we may imitate them
in practicing the virtues of family life and in the bonds of charity,
and so, in the joy of your house,
delight one day in eternal rewards.
Through our Lord Jesus Christ, your Son,
who lives and reigns with you in the unity of the Holy Spirit,
one God, for ever and ever.

(Collect, Feast of the Holy Family)

Reading (*Lectio*)

Read the following Scripture two or three times.
Luke 2:41-52

Each year Jesus' parents went to Jerusalem for the feast of Passover, and when he was twelve years old, they went up according to festival custom. After they had completed its days, as they were returning, the boy Jesus remained behind in Jerusalem, but his parents did not know it. Thinking that he was in the caravan, they journeyed for a day and looked for him among their relatives and acquaintances, but not finding him, they returned to Jerusalem to look for him. After three days they found him in the temple, sitting in the midst of the teachers, listening to them and asking them questions, and all who heard him were astounded at his understanding and his answers. When his parents saw him, they were astonished, and his mother said to him, "Son, why have you done this to us? Your father and I have been looking for you with great anxiety." And he said to them, "Why were you looking for me? Did you not know that I must be in my Father's house?" But they did not understand what he said to them. He went down with them and came to Nazareth, and was obedient to them; and his mother kept all these things in her heart. And Jesus advanced in wisdom and age and favor before God and man.

Meditation (*Meditatio*)

After the reading, take some time to reflect in silence on one or more of the following questions:

- What word or words in this passage caught your attention?
- What in this passage comforted you?
- What in this passage challenged you?

If practicing lectio divina *as a family or in a group, after the reflection time, invite the participants to share their responses.*

Prayer (*Oratio*)

Read the Scripture passage one more time. Bring to the Lord the praise, petition, or thanksgiving that the Word inspires in you.

Contemplation (*Contemplatio*)

Read the Scripture again, followed by this reflection:

What conversion of mind, heart, and life is the Lord asking of me?

They journeyed for a day and looked for him among their relatives and acquaintances. Where do I look for God? How can my friends and family help bring me closer to God?

After three days they found him in the temple, sitting in the midst of the teachers, listening to them and asking them questions. Where do I find God? How do I discern authoritative answers for my questions about faith?

Did you not know that I must be in my Father's house? How can I participate in Mass more fully? What parts of my life can I re-arrange to spend more time in prayer?

After a period of silent reflection and/or discussion, all recite the Lord's Prayer and the following:

Closing Prayer:

How lovely is your dwelling place, O LORD of hosts!
My soul yearns and pines for the courts of the LORD.
My heart and my flesh cry out for the living God.

Happy they who dwell in your house!
  Continually they praise you.
Happy the men whose strength you are!
  Their hearts are set upon the pilgrimage.

O LORD of hosts, hear our prayer;
  hearken, O God of Jacob!
O God, behold our shield,
  and look upon the face of your anointed.

(From Psalm 84)

Living the Word This Week

How can I make my life a gift for others in charity?

Set aside specific time in your calendar to pray and to learn more about your faith, perhaps by reading and reflecting on the *United States Catholic Catechism for Adults.*

Thoughts for Today

January 1, 2019

Lectio Divina for the Solemnity of the Blessed Virgin Mary, Mother of God

We begin our prayer:
In the name of the Father, and of the Son, and of the Holy Spirit.
Amen.

O God, who through the fruitful virginity of Blessed Mary
bestowed on the human race
the grace of eternal salvation,
grant, we pray,
that we may experience the intercession of her,
through whom we were found worthy
to receive the author of life,
our Lord Jesus Christ, your Son.
Who lives and reigns with you in the unity of the Holy Spirit,
one God, for ever and ever.

(Collect, Solemnity of Mary, Mother of God)

Reading (*Lectio*)

Read the following Scripture two or three times.
Luke 2:16-21

The shepherds went in haste to Bethlehem and found Mary and Joseph, and the infant lying in the manger. When they saw this, they made known the message that had been told them about this child. All who heard it were amazed by what had been told them by the shepherds. And Mary kept all these things, reflecting on them in her heart. Then the shepherds returned, glorifying and praising God for all they had heard and seen, just as it had been told to them.

When eight days were completed for his circumcision, he was named Jesus, the name given him by the angel before he was conceived in the womb.

Meditation (*Meditatio*)

After the reading, take some time to reflect in silence on one or more of the following questions:

- What word or words in this passage caught your attention?
- What in this passage comforted you?
- What in this passage challenged you?

If practicing lectio divina *as a family or in a group, after the reflection time, invite the participants to share their responses.*

Prayer (*Oratio*)

Read the Scripture passage one more time. Bring to the Lord the praise, petition, or thanksgiving that the Word inspires in you.

Contemplation (*Contemplatio*)

Read the Scripture again, followed by this reflection:

What conversion of mind, heart, and life is the Lord asking of me?

When they saw this, they made known the message that had been told them about this child. When have I seen God acting in my life? How can I share the message of faith in Jesus Christ in my words and actions?

All who heard it were amazed by what had been told them by the shepherds. When have I been amazed by God working in my life? How can I become more attentive to God's love and mercy acting in my life?

Mary kept all these things, reflecting on them in her heart. Where do I experience challenges in keeping my faith commitments?

How can I make time for silence, prayer, and reflection in my daily schedule?

After a period of silent reflection and/or discussion, all recite the Lord's Prayer and the following:

Closing Prayer:

May God have pity on us and bless us;
  may he let his face shine upon us.
So may your way be known upon earth;
  among all nations, your salvation.

May the nations be glad and exult
  because you rule the peoples in equity;
  the nations on the earth you guide.

May the peoples praise you, O God;
  may all the peoples praise you!
May God bless us,
  and may all the ends of the earth fear him!

(From Psalm 67)

Living the Word This Week

How can I make my life a gift for others in charity?

Make a New Year's resolution to learn more about your faith trough spiritual reading, taking a class, or joining a faith-sharing group.

Thoughts for Today

January 6, 2019

Lectio Divina for the Solemnity of the Epiphany

We begin our prayer:
In the name of the Father, and of the Son, and of the Holy Spirit.
Amen.

O God, who on this day
revealed your Only Begotten Son to the nations
by the guidance of a star,
grant in your mercy, that we, who know you already by faith,
may be brought to behold the beauty of your sublime glory.
Through our Lord Jesus Christ, your Son,
who lives and reigns with you in the unity of the Holy Spirit,
one God, for ever and ever.

(Collect, Epiphany, Mass During the Day)

Reading (*Lectio*)

Read the following Scripture two or three times.
Matthew 2:1-12
When Jesus was born in Bethlehem of Judea, in the days of King Herod, behold, magi from the east arrived in Jerusalem, saying, "Where is the newborn king of the Jews? We saw his star at its rising and have come to do him homage." When King Herod heard this, he was greatly troubled, and all Jerusalem with him. Assembling all the chief priests and the scribes of the people, He inquired of them where the Christ was to be born. They said to him, "In Bethlehem of Judea, for thus it has been written through the prophet:

And you, Bethlehem, land of Judah,
are by no means least among the rulers of Judah;

since from you shall come a ruler,
who is to shepherd my people Israel."

Then Herod called the magi secretly and ascertained from them the time of the star's appearance. He sent them to Bethlehem and said, "Go and search diligently for the child. When you have found him, bring me word, that I too may go and do him homage." After their audience with the king they set out. And behold, the star that they had seen at its rising preceded them, until it came and stopped over the place where the child was. They were overjoyed at seeing the star, and on entering the house they saw the child with Mary his mother. They prostrated themselves and did him homage. Then they opened their treasures and offered him gifts of gold, frankincense, and myrrh. And having been warned in a dream not to return to Herod, they departed for their country by another way.

Meditation (*Meditatio*)

After the reading, take some time to reflect in silence on one or more of the following questions:

- What word or words in this passage caught your attention?
- What in this passage comforted you?
- What in this passage challenged you?

If practicing lectio divina *as a family or in a group, after the reflection time, invite the participants to share their responses.*

Prayer (*Oratio*)

Read the Scripture passage one more time. Bring to the Lord the praise, petition, or thanksgiving that the Word inspires in you.

Contemplation (*Contemplatio*)

Read the Scripture again, followed by this reflection:

What conversion of mind, heart, and life is the Lord asking of me?

We saw his star at its rising and have come to do him homage. For what do I give homage to God? How do I show God my love and gratitude?

You, Bethlehem, land of Judah, / are by no means least among the rulers of Judah. Who is least in my community? How can I be more attentive to those who are often disregarded and at the peripheries?

And behold, the star that they had seen at its rising preceded them, until it came and stopped over the place where the child was. Who has helped lead me to Christ? How do I lead others to him?

After a period of silent reflection and/or discussion, all recite the Lord's Prayer and the following:

Closing Prayer:

O God, with your judgment endow the king,
and with your justice, the king's son;
He shall govern your people with justice
and your afflicted ones with judgment.

Justice shall flower in his days,
and profound peace, till the moon be no more.
May he rule from sea to sea,
and from the River to the ends of the earth.

The kings of Tarshish and the Isles shall offer gifts;
the kings of Arabia and Seba shall bring tribute.
All kings shall pay him homage,
all nations shall serve him.

For he shall rescue the poor when he cries out,
and the afflicted when he has no one to help him.
He shall have pity for the lowly and the poor;
the lives of the poor he shall save.

(From Psalm 72)

Living the Word This Week

How can I make my life a gift for others in charity?

Spend an hour in silent adoration before the Blessed Sacrament, giving God honor and praise.

Thoughts for Today

January 13, 2019

Lectio Divina for the Baptism of the Lord (First Week in Ordinary Time)

We begin our prayer:
In the name of the Father, and of the Son, and of the Holy Spirit.
Amen.

O God, whose Only Begotten Son
has appeared in our very flesh,
grant, we pray, that we may be inwardly transformed
through him whom we recognize as outwardly like ourselves.
Who lives and reigns with you in the unity of the Holy Spirit,
one God, for ever and ever.

(Collect, Baptism of the Lord)

Reading (*Lectio*)

Read the following Scripture two or three times.
Luke 3:15-16, 21-22

The people were filled with expectation, and all were asking in their hearts whether John might be the Christ. John answered them all, saying, "I am baptizing you with water, but one mightier than I is coming. I am not worthy to loosen the thongs of his sandals. He will baptize you with the Holy Spirit and fire."

After all the people had been baptized and Jesus also had been baptized and was praying, heaven was opened and the Holy Spirit descended upon him in bodily form like a dove. And a voice came from heaven, "You are my beloved Son; with you I am well pleased."

Meditation (*Meditatio*)

After the reading, take some time to reflect in silence on one or more of the following questions:

- What word or words in this passage caught your attention?
- What in this passage comforted you?
- What in this passage challenged you?

If practicing lectio divina *as a family or in a group, after the reflection time, invite the participants to share their responses.*

Prayer (*Oratio*)

Read the Scripture passage one more time. Bring to the Lord the praise, petition, or thanksgiving that the Word inspires in you.

Contemplation (*Contemplatio*)

Read the Scripture again, followed by this reflection:

What conversion of mind, heart, and life is the Lord asking of me?

The people were filled with expectation, and all were asking in their hearts whether John might be the Christ. How do I expect God to be present in my life? Do these expectations help or hinder my ability to live faithfully?

I am not worthy to loosen the thongs of his sandals. How can I grow in humility? How can I be of greater service to the people around me?

You are my beloved Son; with you I am well pleased. When have I been most aware of God's love for me? How can I see the people I meet through God's loving eyes?

After a period of silent reflection and/or discussion, all recite the Lord's Prayer and the following:

Closing Prayer:

O Lord, my God, you are great indeed!
  you are clothed with majesty and glory,
robed in light as with a cloak.
  You have spread out the heavens like a tent-cloth;

You have constructed your palace upon the waters.
  You make the clouds your chariot;
you travel on the wings of the wind.
  You make the winds your messengers,
and flaming fire your ministers.

How manifold are your works, O Lord!
  In wisdom you have wrought them all—
the earth is full of your creatures;
  the sea also, great and wide,
in which are schools without number
  of living things both small and great.

They look to you to give them food in due time.
  When you give it to them, they gather it;
when you open your hand, they are filled with good things.

If you take away their breath, they perish and return to the dust.
  When you send forth your spirit, they are created,
and you renew the face of the earth.

(From Psalm 104)

Living the Word This Week

How can I make my life a gift for others in charity?

Renew your baptismal promises by reciting the Apostles' Creed.

Thoughts for Today

January 20, 2019

Lectio Divina for the Second Week in Ordinary Time

We begin our prayer:
In the name of the Father, and of the Son, and of the Holy Spirit. Amen.

Almighty ever-living God,
who govern all things,
both in heaven and on earth,
mercifully hear the pleading of your people
and bestow your peace on our times.
Through our Lord Jesus Christ, your Son,
who lives and reigns with you in the unity of the Holy Spirit,
one God, for ever and ever.

(Collect, Second Sunday in Ordinary Time)

Reading (*Lectio*)

Read the following Scripture two or three times.
John 2:1-11

There was a wedding at Cana in Galilee, and the mother of Jesus was there. Jesus and his disciples were also invited to the wedding. When the wine ran short, the mother of Jesus said to him, "They have no wine." And Jesus said to her, "Woman, how does your concern affect me? My hour has not yet come." His mother said to the servers, "Do whatever he tells you." Now there were six stone water jars there for Jewish ceremonial washings, each holding twenty to thirty gallons. Jesus told the them, "Fill the jars with water." So they filled them to the brim. Then he told them, "Draw some out now and take it to the headwaiter." So they took it. And when the headwaiter tasted the water that had become wine, without knowing where it came from—although the servers who had drawn the water knew—, the headwaiter called the bridegroom and said to him, "Everyone serves good wine first, and then when people have drunk freely, an inferior one; but you have kept the good wine until now." Jesus did this as the beginning of his signs at Cana in Galilee and so revealed his glory, and his disciples began to believe in him.

Meditation (*Meditatio*)

After the reading, take some time to reflect in silence on one or more of the following questions:

- What word or words in this passage caught your attention?
- What in this passage comforted you?
- What in this passage challenged you?

If practicing lectio divina *as a family or in a group, after the reflection time, invite the participants to share their responses.*

Prayer (*Oratio*)

Read the Scripture passage one more time. Bring to the Lord the praise, petition, or thanksgiving that the Word inspires in you.

Contemplation (*Contemplatio*)

Read the Scripture again, followed by this reflection:

What conversion of mind, heart, and life is the Lord asking of me?

Woman, how does your concern affect me? What concerns do I need to bring to the Lord? How can I act to help ease the concerns of others?

Do whatever he tells you. When have I done things against the law of God? When have I failed to do the things I should do?

Jesus did this as the beginning of his signs at Cana in Galilee and so revealed his glory, and his disciples began to believe in him. How have I experience the power and glory of God? What strengthens my faith in God?

After a period of silent reflection and/or discussion, all recite the Lord's Prayer and the following:

Closing Prayer:

Sing to the LORD a new song;
  sing to the LORD, all you lands.
Sing to the LORD; bless his name.

Announce his salvation, day after day.
Tell his glory among the nations;
  among all peoples, his wondrous deeds.

Give to the LORD, you families of nations,
  give to the LORD glory and praise;
  give to the LORD the glory due his name!

  Worship the LORD in holy attire.
Tremble before him, all the earth;
  Say among the nations: The LORD is king.
He governs the peoples with equity.

(From Psalm 96)

Living the Word This Week

How can I make my life a gift for others in charity?

Pray the Rosary (alone or with your family) and ask for the strength to follow Mary's model of discipleship and openness to the will of God.

Thoughts for Today

January 27, 2019

Lectio Divina for the Third Week in Ordinary Time

We begin our prayer:
In the name of the Father, and of the Son, and of the Holy Spirit. Amen.

Almighty ever-living God,
direct our actions according to your good pleasure,
that in the name of your beloved Son
we may abound in good works.
Through our Lord Jesus Christ, your Son,
who lives and reigns with you in the unity of the Holy Spirit,
one God, for ever and ever.

(Collect, Third Sunday in Ordinary Time)

Reading (*Lectio*)

Read the following Scripture two or three times.
Luke 1:1-4; 4:14-21

Since many have undertaken to compile a narrative of the events that have been fulfilled among us, just as those who were eyewitnesses from the beginning and ministers of the word have handed them down to us, I too have decided, after investigating everything accurately anew, to write it down in an orderly sequence for you, most excellent Theophilus, so that you may realize the certainty of the teachings you have received.

Jesus returned to Galilee in the power of the Spirit, and news of him spread throughout the whole region. He taught in their synagogues and was praised by all.

He came to Nazareth, where he had grown up, and went according to his custom into the synagogue on the sabbath day. He stood up to read and was handed a scroll of the prophet Isaiah. He unrolled the scroll and found the passage where it was written:

The Spirit of the Lord is upon me,
because he has anointed me
to bring glad tidings to the poor.
He has sent me to proclaim liberty to captives
and recovery of sight to the blind,
to let the oppressed go free,
and to proclaim a year acceptable to the Lord.

Rolling up the scroll, he handed it back to the attendant and sat down, and the eyes of all in the synagogue looked intently at him. He said to them, "Today this Scripture passage is fulfilled in your hearing."

Meditation (*Meditatio*)

After the reading, take some time to reflect in silence on one or more of the following questions:

- What word or words in this passage caught your attention?
- What in this passage comforted you?
- What in this passage challenged you?

If practicing lectio divina *as a family or in a group, after the reflection time, invite the participants to share their responses.*

Prayer (*Oratio*)

Read the Scripture passage one more time. Bring to the Lord the praise, petition, or thanksgiving that the Word inspires in you.

Contemplation (*Contemplatio*)

Read the Scripture again, followed by this reflection:

What conversion of mind, heart, and life is the Lord asking of me?

Those who were eyewitnesses from the beginning and ministers of the word have handed them down to us. How do I share the Word of God with others? How do I help to hand on the faith to children, family members, friends, etc.?

He . . . went according to his custom into the synagogue on the sabbath day. How do I keep the sabbath? What types of prayer and devotion are customary for me?

The Spirit of the Lord is upon me, / because he has anointed me / to bring glad tidings to the poor. When have I felt the presence of the Spirit most strongly? How can I bring glad tidings to the poor?

After a period of silent reflection and/or discussion, all recite the Lord's Prayer and the following:

Closing Prayer:

The law of the LORD is perfect,
refreshing the soul;
The decree of the LORD is trustworthy,
giving wisdom to the simple.

The precepts of the LORD are right,
rejoicing the heart;
The command of the LORD is clear,
enlightening the eye.

The fear of the LORD is pure,
enduring forever;
The ordinances of the LORD are true,
all of them just.

Let the words of my mouth and the thought of my heart
find favor before you,
O Lord, my rock and my redeemer.

(From Psalm 19)

Living the Word This Week

How can I make my life a gift for others in charity?

Research the work of your parish social justice committee or other charitable endeavor and find a way to accompany the poor and those on the peripheries.

Thoughts for Today

February 3, 2019

Lectio Divina for the Fourth Week in Ordinary Time

We begin our prayer:
In the name of the Father, and of the Son, and of the Holy Spirit.
Amen.

Grant us, Lord our God,
that we may honor you with all our mind,
and love everyone in truth of heart.
Through our Lord Jesus Christ, your Son,
who lives and reigns with you in the unity of the Holy Spirit,
one God, for ever and ever.

(Collect, Fourth Sunday in Ordinary Time)

Reading (*Lectio*)

Read the following Scripture two or three times.
Luke 4:21-30

Jesus began speaking in the synagogue, saying: "Today this Scripture passage is fulfilled in your hearing." And all spoke highly of him and were amazed at the gracious words that came from his mouth. They also asked, "Isn't this the son of Joseph?" He said to them, "Surely you will quote me this proverb, 'Physician, cure yourself,' and say, 'Do here in your native place the things that we heard were done in Capernaum.'" And he said, "Amen, I say to you, no prophet is accepted in his own native place. Indeed, I tell you, there were many widows in Israel in the days of Elijah when the sky was closed for three and a half years and a severe famine spread over the entire land. It was to none of these that Elijah was sent, but only to a widow in Zarephath in the land of Sidon. Again, there were many lepers in Israel during the time of Elisha the prophet; yet not one of them was cleansed, but only Naaman the Syrian." When the people in the synagogue heard this, they were all filled with fury. They rose up, drove him out of the town, and led him to the brow of the hill on which their town had been built, to hurl him down headlong. But Jesus passed through the midst of them and went away.

Meditation (*Meditatio*)

After the reading, take some time to reflect in silence on one or more of the following questions:

- What word or words in this passage caught your attention?
- What in this passage comforted you?
- What in this passage challenged you?

If practicing lectio divina *as a family or in a group, after the reflection time, invite the participants to share their responses.*

Prayer (*Oratio*)

Read the Scripture passage one more time. Bring to the Lord the praise, petition, or thanksgiving that the Word inspires in you.

Contemplation (*Contemplatio*)

Read the Scripture again, followed by this reflection:

What conversion of mind, heart, and life is the Lord asking of me?

Today this Scripture passage is fulfilled in your hearing. How have I experienced the fulfillment of God's promise of love and mercy? What role does reading and praying with Scripture play in my prayer life?

And all spoke highly of him and were amazed at the gracious words that came from his mouth. When have I been amazed by God's power and majesty? How do I reflect my faith in my speech?

When the people in the synagogue heard this, they were all filled with fury. In what ways has my faith led to suffering or difficulties? How can I be a force for peace instead of anger?

After a period of silent reflection and/or discussion, all recite the Lord's Prayer and the following:

Closing Prayer:

In you, O LORD, I take refuge;
  let me never be put to shame.
In your justice rescue me, and deliver me;
  incline your ear to me, and save me.

Be my rock of refuge,
  a stronghold to give me safety,
  for you are my rock and my fortress.
O my God, rescue me from the hand of the wicked.

For you are my hope, O Lord;
  my trust, O God, from my youth.
On you I depend from birth;
  from my mother's womb you are my strength.

My mouth shall declare your justice,
  day by day your salvation.
O God, you have taught me from my youth,
  and till the present I proclaim your wondrous deeds.

(From Psalm 71)

Living the Word This Week

How can I make my life a gift for others in charity?

Work to be a force for reconciliation and kindness in your interactions with others in person and on social media.

Thoughts for Today

February 10, 2019

Lectio Divina for the Fifth Week in Ordinary Time

We begin our prayer:
In the name of the Father, and of the Son, and of the Holy Spirit. Amen.

Keep your family safe, O Lord, with unfailing care,
that, relying solely on the hope of heavenly grace,
they may be defended always by your protection.
Through our Lord Jesus Christ, your Son,
who lives and reigns with you in the unity of the Holy Spirit,
one God, for ever and ever.

(Collect, Fifth Sunday in Ordinary Time)

Reading (*Lectio*)

Read the following Scripture two or three times.
Luke 5:1-11

While the crowd was pressing in on Jesus and listening to the word of God, he was standing by the Lake of Gennesaret. He saw two boats there alongside the lake; the fishermen had disembarked and were washing their nets. Getting into one of the boats, the one belonging to Simon, he asked him to put out a short distance from the shore. Then he sat down and taught the crowds from the boat. After he had finished speaking, he said to Simon, "Put out into deep water and lower your nets for a catch." Simon said in reply, "Master, we have worked hard all night and have caught nothing, but at your command I will lower the nets." When they had done this, they caught a great number of fish and their nets were tearing. They signaled to their partners in the other boat to come to help them.

They came and filled both boats so that the boats were in danger of sinking. When Simon Peter saw this, he fell at the knees of Jesus and said, "Depart from me, Lord, for I am a sinful man." For astonishment at the catch of fish they had made seized him and all those with him, and likewise James and John, the sons of Zebedee, who were partners of Simon. Jesus said to Simon, "Do not be afraid; from now on you will be catching men." When they brought their boats to the shore, they left everything and followed him.

Meditation (*Meditatio*)

After the reading, take some time to reflect in silence on one or more of the following questions:

- What word or words in this passage caught your attention?
- What in this passage comforted you?
- What in this passage challenged you?

If practicing lectio divina *as a family or in a group, after the reflection time, invite the participants to share their responses.*

Prayer (*Oratio*)

Read the Scripture passage one more time. Bring to the Lord the praise, petition, or thanksgiving that the Word inspires in you.

Contemplation (*Contemplatio*)

Read the Scripture again, followed by this reflection:

What conversion of mind, heart, and life is the Lord asking of me?

Put out into deep water and lower your nets for a catch. What deep waters is God calling me to? How can I share my faith with those I meet?

Depart from me, Lord, for I am a sinful man. How does my sinfulness separate me from God and his Church? How can I seek reconciliation and mercy?

Do not be afraid; from now on you will be catching men. How does fear keep me from living my faith? How can I live a life of holiness and joy?

After a period of silent reflection and/or discussion, all recite the Lord's Prayer and the following:

Closing Prayer:

I will give thanks to you, O LORD, with all my heart,
for you have heard the words of my mouth;
in the presence of the angels I will sing your praise;
I will worship at your holy temple
and give thanks to your name.

Because of your kindness and your truth;
for you have made great above all things
your name and your promise.
When I called, you answered me;
you built up strength within me.

All the kings of the earth shall give thanks to you, O LORD,
when they hear the words of your mouth;
and they shall sing of the ways of the LORD:
"Great is the glory of the LORD."

Your right hand saves me.
The LORD will complete what he has done for me;
your kindness, O LORD, endures forever;
forsake not the work of your hands.

(From Psalm 138)

Living the Word This Week

How can I make my life a gift for others in charity?

Pray for the intentions of the Holy Father and all called to servant leadership in the Church.

Thoughts for Today

February 17, 2019

Lectio Divina for the Sixth Week in Ordinary Time

We begin our prayer:
In the name of the Father, and of the Son, and of the Holy Spirit. Amen.

O God, who teach us that you abide
in hearts that are just and true,
grant that we may be so fashioned by your grace
as to become a dwelling pleasing to you.
Through our Lord Jesus Christ, your Son,
who lives and reigns with you in the unity of the Holy Spirit,
one God, for ever and ever.

(Collect, Sixth Sunday in Ordinary Time)

Reading (*Lectio*)

Read the following Scripture two or three times.
Luke 6:17, 20-26

Jesus came down with the twelve and stood on a stretch of level ground with a great crowd of his disciples and a large number of the people from all Judea and Jerusalem and the coastal region of Tyre and Sidon. And raising his eyes toward his disciples he said:

"Blessed are you who are poor,
for the kingdom of God is yours.
Blessed are you who are now hungry,
for you will be satisfied.
Blessed are you who are now weeping,
for you will laugh.

Blessed are you when people hate you, and when they exclude and insult you, and denounce your name as evil on account of the Son of Man. Rejoice and leap for joy on that day! Behold, your reward will be great in heaven. For their ancestors treated the prophets in the same way.

But woe to you who are rich,
for you have received your consolation.
Woe to you who are filled now,
for you will be hungry.
Woe to you who laugh now,
for you will grieve and weep.
Woe to you when all speak well of you,
for their ancestors treated the false prophets in this way."

Meditation (*Meditatio*)

After the reading, take some time to reflect in silence on one or more of the following questions:

- What word or words in this passage caught your attention?
- What in this passage comforted you?
- What in this passage challenged you?

If practicing lectio divina *as a family or in a group, after the reflection time, invite the participants to share their responses.*

Prayer (*Oratio*)

Read the Scripture passage one more time. Bring to the Lord the praise, petition, or thanksgiving that the Word inspires in you.

Contemplation (*Contemplatio*)

Read the Scripture again, followed by this reflection:

What conversion of mind, heart, and life is the Lord asking of me?

Blessed are you who are now hungry, / for you will be satisfied. For what do I hunger? How can my actions be a source of sustenance to those in need?

Blessed are you when people hate you, and when they exclude and insult you, and denounce your name as evil on account of the Son of Man. When have I been excluded or denounced because of my faith? How can I improve my ability to speak the truth in love?

But woe to you who are rich, / for you have received your consolation. How can I become more attentive to others' needs? How can I be more generous with my time, treasure, and talent?

After a period of silent reflection and/or discussion, all recite the Lord's Prayer and the following:

Closing Prayer:

Blessed the man who follows not
the counsel of the wicked,
nor walks in the way of sinners,
nor sits in the company of the insolent,
but delights in the law of the LORD
and meditates on his law day and night.

He is like a tree
planted near running water,
that yields its fruit in due season,
and whose leaves never fade.
Whatever he does, prospers.

Not so the wicked, not so;
they are like chaff which the wind drives away.
For the LORD watches over the way of the just,
but the way of the wicked vanishes.

(From Psalm 1)

Living the Word This Week

How can I make my life a gift for others in charity?

Read Pope Francis's Apostolic Exhortation, *Rejoice and Be Glad*, on the call to holiness.

Thoughts for Today

February 24, 2019

Lectio Divina for the Seventh Week in Ordinary Time

We begin our prayer:
In the name of the Father, and of the Son, and of the Holy Spirit. Amen.

Grant, we pray, almighty God,
that, always pondering spiritual things,
we may carry out in both word and deed
that which is pleasing to you.
Through our Lord Jesus Christ, your Son,
who lives and reigns with you in the unity of the Holy Spirit,
one God, for ever and ever.

(Collect, Seventh Sunday in Ordinary Time)

Reading (*Lectio*)

Read the following Scripture two or three times.
Luke 6:27-38

Jesus said to his disciples: "To you who hear I say, love your enemies, do good to those who hate you, bless those who curse you, pray for those who mistreat you. To the person who strikes you on one cheek, offer the other one as well, and from the person who takes your cloak, do not withhold even your tunic. Give to everyone who asks of you, and from the one who takes what is yours do not demand it back. Do to others as you would have them do to you. For if you love those who love you, what credit is that to you? Even sinners love those who love them. And if you do good to those who do good to you, what credit is that to you? Even sinners do the same. If you lend money to those from whom you expect repayment, what credit is that to you? Even sinners lend to sinners, and get back the same amount. But rather, love your enemies and do good to them, and lend expecting nothing back; then your reward will be great and you will be children of the Most High, for he himself is kind to the ungrateful and the wicked. Be merciful, just as your Father is merciful.

"Stop judging and you will not be judged. Stop condemning and you will not be condemned. Forgive and you will be forgiven. Give, and gifts will be given to you; a good measure, packed together, shaken down, and overflowing, will be poured into your lap. For the measure with which you measure will in return be measured out to you."

Meditation (*Meditatio*)

After the reading, take some time to reflect in silence on one or more of the following questions:

- What word or words in this passage caught your attention?
- What in this passage comforted you?
- What in this passage challenged you?

If practicing lectio divina *as a family or in a group, after the reflection time, invite the participants to share their responses.*

Prayer (*Oratio*)

Read the Scripture passage one more time. Bring to the Lord the praise, petition, or thanksgiving that the Word inspires in you.

Contemplation (*Contemplatio*)

Read the Scripture again, followed by this reflection:

What conversion of mind, heart, and life is the Lord asking of me?

To you who hear I say, love your enemies, do good to those who hate you, bless those who curse you, pray for those who mistreat you. Who are my enemies? How can I best show love to those people?

Give to everyone who asks of you, and from the one who takes what is yours do not demand it back. When do I find it easiest to be generous? Most difficult?

Be merciful, just as your Father is merciful. When was the last time I celebrated God's mercy in the Sacrament of Penance? When was the last time I asked forgiveness of a person I had wronged?

After a period of silent reflection and/or discussion, all recite the Lord's Prayer and the following:

Closing Prayer:

Bless the LORD, O my soul;
  and all my being, bless his holy name.
Bless the LORD, O my soul,
  and forget not all his benefits.

He pardons all your iniquities,
  heals all your ills.
He redeems your life from destruction,
  crowns you with kindness and compassion.

Merciful and gracious is the LORD,
  slow to anger and abounding in kindness.
Not according to our sins does he deal with us,
  nor does he requite us according to our crimes.

As far as the east is from the west,
  so far has he put our transgressions from us.
As a father has compassion on his children,
  so the LORD has compassion on those who fear him.

(From Psalm 103)

Living the Word This Week

How can I make my life a gift for others in charity?

Select a volunteer or donation opportunity in your parish or diocese.

Thoughts for Today

March 3, 2019

Lectio Divina for the Eighth Week in Ordinary Time

We begin our prayer:
In the name of the Father, and of the Son, and of the Holy Spirit.
Amen.

Grant us, O Lord, we pray,
that the course of our world
may be directed by your peaceful rule
and that your Church may rejoice,
untroubled in her devotion.
Through our Lord Jesus Christ, your Son,
who lives and reigns with you in the unity of the Holy Spirit,
one God, for ever and ever.

(Collect, Eighth Sunday in Ordinary Time)

Reading (*Lectio*)

Read the following Scripture two or three times.
Luke 6:39-45

Jesus told his disciples a parable, "Can a blind person guide a blind person? Will not both fall into a pit? No disciple is superior to the teacher; but when fully trained, every disciple will be like his teacher. Why do you notice the splinter in your brother's eye, but do not perceive the wooden beam in your own? How can you say to your brother, 'Brother, let me remove that splinter in your eye,' when you do not even notice the wooden beam in your own eye? You hypocrite! Remove the wooden beam from your eye first; then you will see clearly to remove the splinter in your brother's eye.

"A good tree does not bear rotten fruit, nor does a rotten tree bear good fruit. For every tree is known by its own fruit. For people do not pick figs from thornbushes, nor do they gather grapes from brambles. A good person out of the store of goodness in his heart produces good, but an evil person out of a store of evil produces evil; for from the fullness of the heart the mouth speaks."

Meditation (*Meditatio*)

After the reading, take some time to reflect in silence on one or more of the following questions:

- What word or words in this passage caught your attention?
- What in this passage comforted you?
- What in this passage challenged you?

If practicing lectio divina *as a family or in a group, after the reflection time, invite the participants to share their responses.*

Prayer (*Oratio*)

Read the Scripture passage one more time. Bring to the Lord the praise, petition, or thanksgiving that the Word inspires in you.

Contemplation (*Contemplatio*)

Read the Scripture again, followed by this reflection:

What conversion of mind, heart, and life is the Lord asking of me?

No disciple is superior to the teacher; but when fully trained, every disciple will be like his teacher. What am I doing to increase my knowledge of the faith? How can I better share my faith with my family and friends?

A good tree does not bear rotten fruit, nor does a rotten tree bear good fruit. How do I distinguish between good and bad fruit? What fruit is my life bearing?

From the fullness of the heart the mouth speaks. Are my words kind and true? Do I take opportunities to express my gratitude, love, and concern?

After a period of silent reflection and/or discussion, all recite the Lord's Prayer and the following:

Closing Prayer:

It is good to give thanks to the LORD,
  to sing praise to your name, Most High,
To proclaim your kindness at dawn
  and your faithfulness throughout the night.

The just one shall flourish like the palm tree,
  like a cedar of Lebanon shall he grow.
They that are planted in the house of the LORD
  shall flourish in the courts of our God.

They shall bear fruit even in old age;
  vigorous and sturdy shall they be,
Declaring how just is the LORD,
  my rock, in whom there is no wrong.

(From Psalm 92)

Living the Word This Week

How can I make my life a gift for others in charity?

Commit to a faith formation program in your parish or diocese so that you can learn more.

Thoughts for Today

March 6, 2019

Lectio Divina for Ash Wednesday

We begin our prayer:
In the name of the Father, and of the Son, and of the Holy Spirit. Amen.

Grant, O Lord, that we may begin with holy fasting
this campaign of Christian service,
so that, as we take up battle against spiritual evils,
we may be armed with weapons of self-restraint.
Through our Lord Jesus Christ, your Son,
who lives and reigns with you in the unity of the Holy Spirit,
one God, for ever and ever.

(Collect, Ash Wednesday)

Reading (*Lectio*)

Read the following Scripture two or three times.
Matthew 6:1-6, 16-18

Jesus said to his disciples: "Take care not to perform righteous deeds in order that people may see them; otherwise, you will have no recompense from your heavenly Father. When you give alms, do not blow a trumpet before you, as the hypocrites do in the synagogues and in the streets give alms, do not let your left hand know what your right is doing, so that your almsgiving may be secret. And your Father who sees in secret will repay you.

"When you pray, do not be like the hypocrites, who love to stand and pray in the synagogues and on street corners so that others may see them. Amen, I say to you, they have received their reward. But when you pray, go to your inner room, close the door, and pray to your Father in secret. And your Father who sees in secret will repay you.

"When you fast, do not look gloomy like the hypocrites. They neglect their appearance, so that they may appear to others to be fasting. Amen, I say to you, they have received their reward. But when you fast, anoint your head and wash your face, so that you may not appear to be fasting, except to your Father who is hidden. And your Father who sees what is hidden will repay you."

Meditation (*Meditatio*)

After the reading, take some time to reflect in silence on one or more of the following questions:

- What word or words in this passage caught your attention?
- What in this passage comforted you?
- What in this passage challenged you?

If practicing lectio divina *as a family or in a group, after the reflection time, invite the participants to share their responses.*

Prayer (*Oratio*)

Read the Scripture passage one more time. Bring to the Lord the praise, petition, or thanksgiving that the Word inspires in you.

Contemplation (*Contemplatio*)

Read the Scripture again, followed by this reflection:

What conversion of mind, heart, and life is the Lord asking of me?

But when you pray, go to your inner room, close the door, and pray to your Father in secret. Where is my favorite place to pray? What type of prayer do I want to learn more about?

When you fast, do not look gloomy like the hypocrites. How can I learn greater humility in this Lenten season? How can I share the joy of the Gospel with the people I meet?

And your Father who sees what is hidden will repay you. What needs and intentions are hidden in the secret recesses of my heart? What grace do I need from God today?

After a period of silent reflection and/or discussion, all recite the Lord's Prayer and the following:

Closing Prayer:

Have mercy on me, O God, in your goodness;
in the greatness of your compassion wipe out my offense.
Thoroughly wash me from my guilt
and of my sin cleanse me.

For I acknowledge my offense,
and my sin is before me always:
"Against you only have I sinned,
and done what is evil in your sight."

A clean heart create for me, O God,
and a steadfast spirit renew within me.
Cast me not out from your presence,
and your Holy Spirit take not from me.

Give me back the joy of your salvation,
and a willing spirit sustain in me.
O Lord, open my lips,
and my mouth shall proclaim your praise.

(From Psalm 51)

Living the Word This Week

How can I make my life a gift for others in charity?

Decide what type of prayer, fasting, and almsgiving you will do during this Lenten season.

Thoughts for Today

March 10, 2019

Lectio Divina for the First Week of Lent

We begin our prayer:
In the name of the Father, and of the Son, and of the Holy Spirit.
Amen.

Grant, almighty God,
through the yearly observances of holy Lent,
that we may grow in understanding
of the riches hidden in Christ
and by worthy conduct pursue their effects.
Through our Lord Jesus Christ, your Son,
who lives and reigns with you in the unity of the Holy Spirit,
one God, for ever and ever.

(Collect, First Sunday of Lent)

Reading (*Lectio*)

Read the following Scripture two or three times.
Luke 4:1-14

Filled with the Holy Spirit, Jesus returned from the Jordan and was led by the Spirit into the desert for forty days, to be tempted by the devil. He ate nothing during those days, and when they were over he was hungry. The devil said to him, "If you are the Son of God, command this stone to become bread." Jesus answered him, "It is written, *One does not live on bread alone.*" Then he took him up and showed him all the kingdoms of the world in a single instant. The devil said to him, "I shall give to you all this power and glory; for it has been handed over to me, and I may give it to whomever I wish.

All this will be yours, if you worship me." Jesus said to him in reply, "It is written:

You shall worship the Lord, your God,
and him alone shall you serve."

Then he led him to Jerusalem, made him stand on the parapet of the temple, and said to him, "If you are the Son of God, throw yourself down from here, for it is written:

He will command his angels concerning you, to guard you,

and:

With their hands they will support you,
lest you dash your foot against a stone."

Jesus said to him in reply, "It also says, *You shall not put the Lord, your God, to the test.*" When the devil had finished every temptation, he departed from him for a time.

Meditation (*Meditatio*)

After the reading, take some time to reflect in silence on one or more of the following questions:

- What word or words in this passage caught your attention?
- What in this passage comforted you?
- What in this passage challenged you?

If practicing lectio divina *as a family or in a group, after the reflection time, invite the participants to share their responses.*

Prayer (*Oratio*)

Read the Scripture passage one more time. Bring to the Lord the praise, petition, or thanksgiving that the Word inspires in you.

Contemplation (*Contemplatio*)

Read the Scripture again, followed by this reflection:

What conversion of mind, heart, and life is the Lord asking of me?

Jesus returned from the Jordan and was led by the Spirit into the desert for forty days, to be tempted by the devil. When have I been tempted away from a life of faith? Where are the deserts in my faith life?

One does not live on bread alone. What spiritual practices nourish my faith? How can I place God at the center of my life?

You shall not put the Lord, your God, to the test. When is my faith in God tested most strongly? How can I support others when they face trials?

After a period of silent reflection and/or discussion, all recite the Lord's Prayer and the following:

Closing Prayer:

You who dwell in the shelter of the Most High,
 who abide in the shadow of the Almighty,
say to the LORD, "My refuge and fortress,
 my God in whom I trust."

No evil shall befall you,
 nor shall affliction come near your tent,
For to his angels he has given command about you,
 that they guard you in all your ways.

Upon their hands they shall bear you up,
 lest you dash your foot against a stone.
You shall tread upon the asp and the viper;
 you shall trample down the lion and the dragon.

Because he clings to me, I will deliver him;
 I will set him on high because he acknowledges my name.
He shall call upon me, and I will answer him;

I will be with him in distress;
I will deliver him and glorify him.

(From Psalm 91)

Living the Word This Week

How can I make my life a gift for others in charity?

Make plans to receive the Sacrament of Penance during Lent.

Thoughts for Today

March 17, 2019

Lectio Divina for the Second Week of Lent

We begin our prayer:
In the name of the Father, and of the Son, and of the Holy Spirit. Amen.

O God, who have commanded us
to listen to your beloved Son,
be pleased, we pray,
to nourish us inwardly by your word,
that, with spiritual sight made pure,
we may rejoice to behold your glory.
Through our Lord Jesus Christ, your Son,
who lives and reigns with you in the unity of the Holy Spirit,
one God, for ever and ever.

(Collect, Second Sunday of Lent)

Reading (*Lectio*)

Read the following Scripture two or three times.
Luke 9:28b-36

Jesus took Peter, John, and James and went up the mountain to pray. While he was praying his face changed in appearance and his clothing became dazzling white. And behold, two men were conversing with him, Moses and Elijah, who appeared in glory and spoke of his exodus that he was going to accomplish in Jerusalem. Peter and his companions had been overcome by sleep, but becoming fully awake, they saw his glory and the two men standing with him. As they were about to part from him, Peter said to Jesus, "Master, it is good that we are here; let us make three tents, one for you, one for Moses, and one for Elijah." But he did not know what he was saying.

While he was still speaking, a cloud came and cast a shadow over them, and they became frightened when they entered the cloud. Then from the cloud came a voice that said, "This is my chosen Son; listen to him." After the voice had spoken, Jesus was found alone. They fell silent and did not at that time tell anyone what they had seen.

Meditation (*Meditatio*)

After the reading, take some time to reflect in silence on one or more of the following questions:

- What word or words in this passage caught your attention?
- What in this passage comforted you?
- What in this passage challenged you?

If practicing lectio divina *as a family or in a group, after the reflection time, invite the participants to share their responses.*

Prayer (*Oratio*)

Read the Scripture passage one more time. Bring to the Lord the praise, petition, or thanksgiving that the Word inspires in you.

Contemplation (*Contemplatio*)

Read the Scripture again, followed by this reflection:

What conversion of mind, heart, and life is the Lord asking of me?

Jesus took Peter, John, and James and went up the mountain to pray. Where do I like to pray? What are the benefits and challenges of praying alone and with others?

Becoming fully awake, they saw his glory. What people, places, or things make me more likely to be aware of God's will? How can I be more attentive to God's presence in my life?

They fell silent and did not at that time tell anyone what they had seen. What fears keep me from sharing my faith with others? What fears keep me from living my faith in the public square?

After a period of silent reflection and/or discussion, all recite the Lord's Prayer and the following:

Closing Prayer:

The LORD is my light and my salvation;
  whom should I fear?
The LORD is my life's refuge;
  of whom should I be afraid?

Hear, O LORD, the sound of my call;
  have pity on me, and answer me.
Of you my heart speaks; you my glance seeks.

Your presence, O LORD, I seek.
  Hide not your face from me;
do not in anger repel your servant.
  You are my helper: cast me not off.

I believe that I shall see the bounty of the LORD
  in the land of the living.
Wait for the LORD with courage;
  be stouthearted, and wait for the LORD.

(From Psalm 27)

Living the Word This Week

How can I make my life a gift for others in charity?

Read *Disciples Called to Witness* about the new evangelization:

http://www.usccb.org/beliefs-and-teachings/how-we-teach/new-evangelization/disciples-called-to-witness/upload/Disciples-Called-to-Witness-5-30-12.pdf.

Thoughts for Today

March 24, 2019

Lectio Divina for the Third Week of Lent

We begin our prayer:
In the name of the Father, and of the Son, and of the Holy Spirit.
Amen.

O God, author of every mercy and of all goodness,
who in fasting, prayer and almsgiving
have shown us a remedy for sin,
look graciously on this confession of our lowliness,
that we, who are bowed down by our conscience,
may always be lifted up by your mercy.
Through our Lord Jesus Christ, your Son,
who lives and reigns with you in the unity of the Holy Spirit,
one God, for ever and ever.

(Collect, Third Sunday of Lent)

Reading (*Lectio*)

Read the following Scripture two or three times.
Luke 13:1-9

Some people told Jesus about the Galileans whose blood Pilate had mingled with the blood of their sacrifices. Jesus said to them in reply, "Do you think that because these Galileans suffered in this way they were greater sinners than all other Galileans? By no means! But I tell you, if you do not repent, you will all perish as they did! Or those eighteen people who were killed when the tower at Siloam fell on them—do you think they were more guilty than everyone else who lived in Jerusalem? By no means! But I tell you, if you do not repent, you will all perish as they did!"

And he told them this parable: "There once was a person who had a fig tree planted in his orchard, and when he came in search of fruit on it but found none, he said to the gardener, 'For three years now I have come in search of fruit on this fig tree but have found none. So cut it down. Why should it exhaust the soil?' He said to him in reply, 'Sir, leave it for this year also, and I shall cultivate the ground around it and fertilize it; it may bear fruit in the future. If not you can cut it down.'"

Meditation (*Meditatio*)

After the reading, take some time to reflect in silence on one or more of the following questions:

- What word or words in this passage caught your attention?
- What in this passage comforted you?
- What in this passage challenged you?

If practicing lectio divina *as a family or in a group, after the reflection time, invite the participants to share their responses.*

Prayer (*Oratio*)

Read the Scripture passage one more time. Bring to the Lord the praise, petition, or thanksgiving that the Word inspires in you.

Contemplation (*Contemplatio*)

Read the Scripture again, followed by this reflection:

What conversion of mind, heart, and life is the Lord asking of me?

If you do not repent, you will all perish as they did! What sinful practices are hurting my faith? How can I amend my life to live by God's law?

He came in search of fruit on it but found none. Where do I search for fruit to nourish my spiritual life? How can I help those who search for peace to find God?

I shall cultivate the ground around it and fertilize it; it may bear fruit in the future. How can I cultivate a closer relationship with Jesus? How am I called to bear fruit for the kingdom of God?

After a period of silent reflection and/or discussion, all recite the Lord's Prayer and the following:

Closing Prayer:

Bless the LORD, O my soul;
  and all my being, bless his holy name.
Bless the LORD, O my soul,
  and forget not all his benefits.

He pardons all your iniquities,
  heals all your ills,
He redeems your life from destruction,
  crowns you with kindness and compassion.

The LORD secures justice
  and the rights of all the oppressed.
He has made known his ways to Moses,
  and his deeds to the children of Israel.

Merciful and gracious is the LORD,
  slow to anger and abounding in kindness.
For as the heavens are high above the earth,
  so surpassing is his kindness toward those who fear him.

(From Psalm 103)

Living the Word This Week

How can I make my life a gift for others in charity?

Pray for the Church's ministry to our poor and vulnerable brothers and sisters around the world (*ww.crs.org*).

Thoughts for Today

March 31, 2019

Lectio Divina for the Fourth Week of Lent

We begin our prayer:
In the name of the Father, and of the Son, and of the Holy Spirit. Amen.

O God, who through your Word
reconcile the human race to yourself in a wonderful way,
grant, we pray,
that with prompt devotion and eager faith
the Christian people may hasten
toward the solemn celebrations to come.
Through our Lord Jesus Christ, your Son,
who lives and reigns with you in the unity of the Holy Spirit,
one God, for ever and ever.

(Collect, Fourth Sunday of Lent)

Reading (*Lectio*)

Read the following Scripture two or three times.
Luke 15:1-3, 11-32

Tax collectors and sinners were all drawing near to listen to Jesus, but the Pharisees and scribes began to complain, saying, "This man welcomes sinners and eats with them." So to them Jesus addressed this parable: "A man had two sons, and the younger son said to his father, 'Father give me the share of your estate that should come to me.'

So the father divided the property between them. After a few days, the younger son collected all his belongings and set off to a distant country where he squandered his inheritance on a life of dissipation. When he had freely spent everything, a severe famine struck that country, and he found himself in dire need. So he hired himself out to one of the local citizens who sent him to his farm to tend the swine. And he longed to eat his fill of the pods on which the swine fed, but nobody gave him any. Coming to his senses he thought, 'How many of my father's hired workers have more than enough food to eat, but here am I, dying from hunger. I shall get up and go to my father and I shall say to him, "Father, I have sinned against heaven and against you. I no longer deserve to be called your son; treat me as you would treat one of your hired workers."' So he got up and went back to his father. While he was still a long way off, his father caught sight of him, and was filled with compassion. He ran to his son, embraced him and kissed him. His son said to him, 'Father, I have sinned against heaven and against you; I no longer deserve to be called your son.' But his father ordered his servants, 'Quickly bring the finest robe and put it on him; put a ring on his finger and sandals on his feet. Take the fattened calf and slaughter it. Then let us celebrate with a feast, because this son of mine was dead, and has come to life again; he was lost, and has been found.' Then the celebration began. Now the older son had been out in the field and, on his way back, as he neared the house, he heard the sound of music and dancing. He called one of the servants and asked what this might mean. The servant said to him, 'Your brother has returned and your father has slaughtered the fattened calf because he has him back safe and sound.' He became angry, and when he refused to enter the house, his father came out and pleaded with him. He said to his father in reply, 'Look, all these years I served you and not once did I disobey your orders; yet you never gave me even a young goat to feast on with my friends. But when your son returns who swallowed up your property with prostitutes, for him you slaughter the fattened calf.' He said to him, 'My son, you are here with me always; everything I have is yours. But now we must celebrate and rejoice, because your brother was dead and has come to life again; he was lost and has been found.'"

Meditation (*Meditatio*)

After the reading, take some time to reflect in silence on one or more of the following questions:

- What word or words in this passage caught your attention?
- What in this passage comforted you?
- What in this passage challenged you?

If practicing lectio divina *as a family or in a group, after the reflection time, invite the participants to share their responses.*

Prayer (*Oratio*)

Read the Scripture passage one more time. Bring to the Lord the praise, petition, or thanksgiving that the Word inspires in you.

Contemplation (*Contemplatio*)

Read the Scripture again, followed by this reflection:

What conversion of mind, heart, and life is the Lord asking of me?

This man welcomes sinners and eats with them. Do I seek the mercy of God in regular examination of conscience and recourse to the Sacrament of Penance? How do I welcome fellow sinners with a generous heart?

While he was still a long way off, his father caught sight of him, and was filled with compassion. When have I felt the mercy and compassion of God? How can I witness to God's compassion among those who are lonely and afraid?

He became angry, and . . . he refused to enter the house. When have I refused to extend forgiveness to someone who hurt me? What grudges am I carrying?

After a period of silent reflection and/or discussion, all recite the Lord's Prayer and the following:

Closing Prayer:

I will bless the LORD at all times;
his praise shall be ever in my mouth.
Let my soul glory in the LORD;
the lowly will hear me and be glad.

Glorify the LORD with me,
let us together extol his name.
I sought the LORD, and he answered me
and delivered me from all my fears.

Look to him that you may be radiant with joy,
and your faces may not blush with shame.
When the poor one called out, the LORD heard,
and from all his distress he saved him.

(From Psalm 34)

Living the Word This Week

How can I make my life a gift for others in charity?

Read *God's Gift of Forgiveness: A Pastoral Statement on Penance and Reconciliation:*

http://www.usccb.org/prayer-and-worship/sacraments-and-sacramentals/penance/upload/Penance-Statement-ENG.pdf.

Thoughts for Today

April 7, 2019

Lectio Divina for the Fifth Week of Lent

We begin our prayer:
In the name of the Father, and of the Son, and of the Holy Spirit. Amen.

By your help, we beseech you, Lord our God,
may we walk eagerly in that same charity
with which, out of love for the world,
your Son handed himself over to death.
Through our Lord Jesus Christ, your Son,
who lives and reigns with you in the unity of the Holy Spirit,
one God, for ever and ever.

(Collect, Fifth Sunday of Lent)

Reading (Lectio)

Read the following Scripture two or three times.
John 8:1-11

Jesus went to the Mount of Olives. But early in the morning he arrived again in the temple area, and all the people started coming to him, and he sat down and taught them. Then the scribes and the Pharisees brought a woman who had been caught in adultery and made her stand in the middle. They said to him, "Teacher, this woman was caught in the very act of committing adultery. Now in the law, Moses commanded us to stone such women. So what do you say?"

They said this to test him, so that they could have some charge to bring against him. Jesus bent down and began to write on the ground with his finger. But when they continued asking him, he straightened up and said to them, "Let the one among you who is without sin be the first to throw a stone at her." Again he bent down and wrote on the ground. And in response, they went away one by one, beginning with the elders. So he was left alone with the woman before him. Then Jesus straightened up and said to her, "Woman, where are they? Has no one condemned you?"

She replied, "No one, sir." Then Jesus said, "Neither do I condemn you. Go, and from now on do not sin any more."

Meditation (*Meditatio*)

After the reading, take some time to reflect in silence on one or more of the following questions:

- What word or words in this passage caught your attention?
- What in this passage comforted you?
- What in this passage challenged you?

If practicing lectio divina *as a family or in a group, after the reflection time, invite the participants to share their responses.*

Prayer (*Oratio*)

Read the Scripture passage one more time. Bring to the Lord the praise, petition, or thanksgiving that the Word inspires in you.

Contemplation (*Contemplatio*)

Read the Scripture again, followed by this reflection:

What conversion of mind, heart, and life is the Lord asking of me?

All the people started coming to him, and he sat down and taught them. Where can I find authentic teaching? How can I rearrange my schedule so that I can spend more time learning about my faith?

They said this to test him. How do I try to test God's faithfulness and mercy? How can I deepen my trust in God's providence?

Let the one among you who is without sin be the first to throw a stone. When am I most likely to judge another person? How can I become more aware of my own need for God's mercy?

After a period of silent reflection and/or discussion, all recite the Lord's Prayer and the following:

Closing Prayer:

When the LORD brought back the captives of Zion,
    we were like men dreaming.
Then our mouth was filled with laughter,
    and our tongue with rejoicing.

Then they said among the nations,
    "The LORD has done great things for them."
The LORD has done great things for us;
    we are glad indeed.

Restore our fortunes, O LORD,
    like the torrents in the southern desert.
Those that sow in tears
    shall reap rejoicing.

Although they go forth weeping,
    carrying the seed to be sown,
They shall come back rejoicing,
    carrying their sheaves.

(From Psalm 126)

Living the Word This Week

How can I make my life a gift for others in charity?

Extend forgiveness to someone who has hurt you and ask forgiveness of someone you have hurt.

Thoughts for Today

April 14, 2019

Lectio Divina for Palm Sunday

We begin our prayer:
In the name of the Father, and of the Son, and of the Holy Spirit.
Amen.

Almighty ever-living God,
who as an example of humility for the human race to follow
caused our Savior to take flesh and submit to the Cross,
graciously grant that we may heed his lesson of patient suffering
and so merit a share in his Resurrection.
Who lives and reigns with you in the unity of the Holy Spirit,
one God, for ever and ever.

(Collect, Palm Sunday)

Reading (*Lectio*)

Read the following Scripture two or three times.
Luke 19:28-40

Jesus proceeded on his journey up to Jerusalem. As he drew near to Bethphage and Bethany at the place called the Mount of Olives, he sent two of his disciples. He said, "Go into the village opposite you, and as you enter it you will find a colt tethered on which no one has ever sat. Untie it and bring it here. And if anyone should ask you, 'Why are you untying it?' you will answer, 'The Master has need of it.'" So those who had been sent went off and found everything just as he had told them. And as they were untying the colt, its owners said to them, "Why are you untying this colt?" They answered, "The Master has need of it." So they brought it to Jesus, threw their cloaks over the colt, and helped Jesus to mount. As he rode along, the people were spreading their cloaks on the road; and now as he was approaching the slope of the Mount of Olives, the whole multitude of his disciples began to praise God aloud with joy for all the mighty deeds they had seen. They proclaimed:

> "Blessed is the king who comes
> in the name of the Lord.
> Peace in heaven
> and glory in the highest."

Some of the Pharisees in the crowd said to him, "Teacher, rebuke your disciples." He said in reply, "I tell you, if they keep silent, the stones will cry out!"

Meditation (*Meditatio*)

After the reading, take some time to reflect in silence on one or more of the following questions:

- What word or words in this passage caught your attention?
- What in this passage comforted you?
- What in this passage challenged you?

If practicing lectio divina *as a family or in a group, after the reflection time, invite the participants to share their responses.*

Prayer (*Oratio*)

Read the Scripture passage one more time. Bring to the Lord the praise, petition, or thanksgiving that the Word inspires in you.

Contemplation (*Contemplatio*)

Read the Scripture again, followed by this reflection:

What conversion of mind, heart, and life is the Lord asking of me?

And if anyone should ask you, "Why are you untying it?" you will answer, "The Master has need of it." When have I been challenged about living my faith? How do I respond to those challenges?

The whole multitude of his disciples began to praise God aloud with joy for all the mighty deeds they had seen. What good works has God accomplished in me during this Lenten season? How have I seen God working in my life and in the lives of those around me?

I tell you, if they keep silent, the stones will cry out! When am I silent when I should speak out? How can I be more attentive to the voice of God?

After a period of silent reflection and/or discussion, all recite the Lord's Prayer and the following:

Closing Prayer:

All who see me scoff at me;
  they mock me with parted lips, they wag their heads:
"He relied on the LORD; let him deliver him,
  let him rescue him, if he loves him."

Indeed, many dogs surround me,
  a pack of evildoers closes in upon me;
They have pierced my hands and my feet;
  I can count all my bones.

They divide my garments among them,
  and for my vesture they cast lots.
But you, O LORD, be not far from me;
  O my help, hasten to aid me.

I will proclaim your name to my brethren;
  in the midst of the assembly I will praise you:
"You who fear the LORD, praise him;
  all you descendants of Jacob, give glory to him;
  revere him, all you descendants of Israel!"

(From Psalm 22)

Living the Word This Week

How can I make my life a gift for others in charity?

Make plans to attend your parish's celebration of the Paschal Triduum.

Thoughts for Today

April 21, 2019

Lectio Divina for the Octave of Easter

We begin our prayer:
In the name of the Father, and of the Son, and of the Holy Spirit. Amen.

Almighty ever-living God,
who gave us the Paschal Mystery
in the covenant you established
for reconciling the human race,
so dispose our minds, we pray,
that what we celebrate by professing the faith
we may express in deeds.
Through our Lord Jesus Christ, your Son,
who lives and reigns with you in the unity of the Holy Spirit,
one God, for ever and ever.

(Collect, Friday within the Octave of Easter)

Reading (*Lectio*)

Read the following Scripture two or three times.
Luke 24:1-12

At daybreak on the first day of the week the women who had come from Galilee with Jesus took the spices they had prepared and went to the tomb. They found the stone rolled away from the tomb; but when they entered, they did not find the body of the Lord Jesus. While they were puzzling over this, behold, two men in dazzling garments appeared to them. They were terrified and bowed their faces to the ground. They said to them, "Why do you seek the living one among the dead? He is not here, but he has been raised. Remember what he said to you while he was still in Galilee, that the Son of Man must be handed over to sinners and be crucified, and rise on the third day." And they remembered his words. Then they returned from the tomb and announced all these things to the eleven and to all the others. The women were Mary Magdalene, Joanna, and Mary the mother of James; the others who accompanied them also told this to the apostles, but their story seemed like nonsense and they did not believe them. But Peter got up and ran to the tomb, bent down, and saw the burial cloths alone; then he went home amazed at what had happened.

Meditation (*Meditatio*)

After the reading, take some time to reflect in silence on one or more of the following questions:

- What word or words in this passage caught your attention?
- What in this passage comforted you?
- What in this passage challenged you?

If practicing lectio divina *as a family or in a group, after the reflection time, invite the participants to share their responses.*

Prayer (*Oratio*)

Read the Scripture passage one more time. Bring to the Lord the praise, petition, or thanksgiving that the Word inspires in you.

Contemplation (*Contemplatio*)

Read the Scripture again, followed by this reflection:

What conversion of mind, heart, and life is the Lord asking of me?

While they were puzzling over this, behold, two men in dazzling garments appeared to them. What teachings of the Church do I struggle to understand? Where can I go to get reliable and truthful explanations?

Why do you seek the living one among the dead? He is not here, but he has been raised. Where do I seek Jesus? How does my belief in Jesus' resurrection affect my daily life?

But their story seemed like nonsense and they did not believe them. When has my faith been mocked or discounted? How can I respond to someone who questions my faith?

After a period of silent reflection and/or discussion, all recite the Lord's Prayer and the following:

Closing Prayer:

Give thanks to the LORD, for he is good,
  for his mercy endures forever.
Let the house of Israel say,
  "His mercy endures forever."

"The right hand of the LORD has struck with power;
  the right hand of the LORD is exalted.
I shall not die, but live,
  and declare the works of the LORD."

The stone which the builders rejected
  has become the cornerstone.
By the LORD has this been done;
  it is wonderful in our eyes.

(From Psalm 118)

Living the Word This Week

How can I make my life a gift for others in charity?

Consider joining parish or diocesan evangelization efforts to help spread the Good News of the Resurrection.

Thoughts for Today

April 28, 2019

Lectio Divina for the Second Week of Easter

We begin our prayer:
In the name of the Father, and of the Son, and of the Holy Spirit. Amen.

O God, hope and light of the sincere,
we humbly entreat you to dispose our hearts
to offer you worthy prayer
and ever to extol you
by dutiful proclamation of your praise.
Through our Lord Jesus Christ, your Son,
who lives and reigns with you in the unity of the Holy Spirit,
one God, for ever and ever.

(Collect, Friday of the Second Week of Easter)

Reading (*Lectio*)

Read the following Scripture two or three times.
John 20:19-31

On the evening of that first day of the week, when the doors were locked, where the disciples were, for fear of the Jews, Jesus came and stood in their midst and said to them, "Peace be with you." When he had said this, he showed them his hands and his side. The disciples rejoiced when they saw the Lord. Jesus said to them again, "Peace be with you. As the Father has sent me, so I send you." And when he had said this, he breathed on them and said to them, "Receive the Holy Spirit. Whose sins you forgive are forgiven them, and whose sins you retain are retained."

Thomas, called Didymus, one of the Twelve, was not with them when Jesus came. So the other disciples said to him, "We have seen the Lord." But he said to them, "Unless I see the mark of the nails in his hands and put my finger into the nailmarks and put my hand into his side, I will not believe."

Now a week later his disciples were again inside and Thomas was with them. Jesus came, although the doors were locked, and stood in their midst and said, "Peace be with you." Then he said to Thomas, "Put your finger here and see my hands, and bring your hand and put it into my side, and do not be unbelieving, but believe." Thomas answered and said to him, "My Lord and my God!" Jesus said to him, "Have you come to believe because you have seen me? Blessed are those who have not seen and have believed."

Now Jesus did many other signs in the presence of his disciples that are not written in this book. But these are written that you may come to believe that Jesus is the Christ, the Son of God, and that through this belief you may have life in his name.

Meditation (*Meditatio*)

After the reading, take some time to reflect in silence on one or more of the following questions:

- What word or words in this passage caught your attention?
- What in this passage comforted you?
- What in this passage challenged you?

If practicing lectio divina *as a family or in a group, after the reflection time, invite the participants to share their responses.*

Prayer (*Oratio*)

Read the Scripture passage one more time. Bring to the Lord the praise, petition, or thanksgiving that the Word inspires in you.

Contemplation (*Contemplatio*)

Read the Scripture again, followed by this reflection:

What conversion of mind, heart, and life is the Lord asking of me?

Peace be with you. What parts of my life need more peace? How can I be a force for peace in my family and community?

We have seen the Lord. When have I experienced the presence of the Lord? When have I seen God's hand at work in my life?

But these are written that you may come to believe that Jesus is the Christ, the Son of God. Who introduced me to faith in Christ? How can I share my faith with others?

After a period of silent reflection and/or discussion, all recite the Lord's Prayer and the following:

Closing Prayer:

Let the house of Israel say,
"His mercy endures forever."
Let the house of Aaron say,
"His mercy endures forever."
Let those who fear the LORD say,
"His mercy endures forever."

I was hard pressed and was falling,
but the LORD helped me.
My strength and my courage is the LORD,
and he has been my savior.
The joyful shout of victory
in the tents of the just:

The stone which the builders rejected
has become the cornerstone.
By the LORD has this been done;
it is wonderful in our eyes.
This is the day the LORD has made;
let us be glad and rejoice in it.

(From Psalm 118)

Living the Word This Week

How can I make my life a gift for others in charity?

Become involved in your parish's catechetical ministry, as a participant or a catechist.

Thoughts for Today

May 5, 2019

Lectio Divina for the Third Week of Easter

We begin our prayer:
In the name of the Father, and of the Son, and of the Holy Spirit. Amen.

Grant, we pray, almighty God,
that we, who have come to know
the grace of the Lord's Resurrection,
may, through the love of the Spirit,
ourselves rise to newness of life.
Through our Lord Jesus Christ, your Son,
who lives and reigns with you in the unity of the Holy Spirit,
one God, for ever and ever.

(Collect, Friday of the Third Week of Easter)

Reading (*Lectio*)

Read the following Scripture two or three times.
John 21:1-19

At that time, Jesus revealed himself again to his disciples at the Sea of Tiberias. He revealed himself in this way. Together were Simon Peter, Thomas called Didymus, Nathanael from Cana in Galilee, Zebedee's sons, and two others of his disciples. Simon Peter said to them, "I am going fishing." They said to him, "We also will come with you." So they went out and got into the boat, but that night they caught nothing. When it was already dawn, Jesus was standing on the shore; but the disciples did not realize that it was Jesus. Jesus said to them, "Children, have you caught anything to eat?" They answered him, "No." So he said to them, "Cast the net over the right side of the boat and you will find something." So they cast it, and were not able to pull it in because of the number of fish. So the disciple whom Jesus loved said to Peter, "It is the Lord." When Simon Peter heard that it was the Lord, he tucked in his garment, for he was lightly clad, and jumped into the sea. The other disciples came in the boat, for they were not far from shore, only about a hundred yards, dragging the net with the fish. When they climbed out on shore, they saw a charcoal fire with fish on it and bread. Jesus said to them, "Bring some of the fish you just caught." So Simon Peter went over and dragged the net ashore full of one hundred fifty-three large fish. Even though there were so many, the net was not torn. Jesus said to them, "Come, have breakfast." And none of the disciples dared to ask him, "Who are you?" because they realized it was the Lord. Jesus came over and took the bread and gave it to them, and in like manner the fish. This was now the third time Jesus was revealed to his disciples after being raised from the dead.

When they had finished breakfast, Jesus said to Simon Peter, "Simon, son of John, do you love me more than these?" Simon Peter answered him, "Yes, Lord, you know that I love you." Jesus said to him, "Feed my lambs." He then said to Simon Peter a second time, "Simon, son of John, do you love me?" Simon Peter answered him, "Yes, Lord, you know that I love you." Jesus said to him, "Tend my sheep." Jesus said to him the third time, "Simon, son of John, do you love me?" Peter was distressed that Jesus had said to him a third time, "Do you love me?" and he said to him, "Lord, you know everything; you know that I love you." Jesus said to him, "Feed my sheep. Amen, amen, I say to you, when you were younger, you used to dress yourself and go where you wanted; but when you grow old, you will stretch out your hands, and someone else will dress you and lead you where you do not want to go." He said this signifying by what kind of death he would glorify God. And when he had said this, he said to him, "Follow me."

Meditation (*Meditatio*)

After the reading, take some time to reflect in silence on one or more of the following questions:

- What word or words in this passage caught your attention?
- What in this passage comforted you?
- What in this passage challenged you?

If practicing lectio divina *as a family or in a group, after the reflection time, invite the participants to share their responses.*

Prayer (*Oratio*)

Read the Scripture passage one more time. Bring to the Lord the praise, petition, or thanksgiving that the Word inspires in you.

Contemplation (*Contemplatio*)

Read the Scripture again, followed by this reflection:

What conversion of mind, heart, and life is the Lord asking of me?

The disciples did not realize that it was Jesus. When have I failed to recognize God's presence in my life? When have I failed to see Christ in the people around me, especially those on the peripheries?

Do you love me? Do I love God with my whole heart and mind and soul? How do I show my love for God?

Follow me. Where is Jesus calling me to go? What challenges might I experience in following Jesus?

After a period of silent reflection and/or discussion, all recite the Lord's Prayer and the following:

Closing Prayer:

I will extol you, O Lord, for you drew me clear
  and did not let my enemies rejoice over me.
O Lord, you brought me up from the netherworld;

you preserved me from among those going down into the pit.

Sing praise to the LORD, you his faithful ones,
and give thanks to his holy name.
For his anger lasts but a moment;
a lifetime, his good will.
At nightfall, weeping enters in,
but with the dawn, rejoicing.

Hear, O LORD, and have pity on me;
O LORD, be my helper.
You changed my mourning into dancing;
O LORD, my God, forever will I give you thanks.

(From Psalm 30)

Living the Word This Week

How can I make my life a gift for others in charity?

Participate in a parish social justice project and pray for the people who are served.

Thoughts for Today

May 12, 2019

Lectio Divina for the Fourth Week of Easter

We begin our prayer:
In the name of the Father, and of the Son, and of the Holy Spirit. Amen.

O God, life of the faithful,
glory of the humble, blessedness of the just,
listen kindly to the prayers
of those who call on you,
that they who thirst for what you generously promise
may always have their fill of your plenty.
Through our Lord Jesus Christ, your Son,
who lives and reigns with you in the unity of the Holy Spirit,
one God, for ever and ever.

(Collect, Wednesday of the Fourth Week of Easter)

Reading (*Lectio*)

Read the following Scripture two or three times.
John 10: 27-30

Jesus said: "My sheep hear my voice; I know them, and they follow me. I give them eternal life, and they shall never perish. No one can take them out of my hand. My Father, who has given them to me, is greater than all, and no one can take them out of the Father's hand. The Father and I are one."

Meditation (*Meditatio*)

After the reading, take some time to reflect in silence on one or more of the following questions:

- What word or words in this passage caught your attention?
- What in this passage comforted you?
- What in this passage challenged you?

If practicing lectio divina *as a family or in a group, after the reflection time, invite the participants to share their responses.*

Prayer (*Oratio*)

Read the Scripture passage one more time. Bring to the Lord the praise, petition, or thanksgiving that the Word inspires in you.

Contemplation (*Contemplatio*)

Read the Scripture again, followed by this reflection:

What conversion of mind, heart, and life is the Lord asking of me?

My sheep hear my voice. Where do I go to hear the voice of God? How can I be more attentive to God's voice?

I know them, and they follow me. How have I encountered Jesus? How does this encounter change the way I live?

The Father and I are one. What can I do to grow close to God? How can I be a force for unity rather than division?

After a period of silent reflection and/or discussion, all recite the Lord's Prayer and the following:

Closing Prayer:

Sing joyfully to the LORD, all you lands;
serve the LORD with gladness;
come before him with joyful song.

Know that the LORD is God;
  he made us, his we are;
  his people, the flock he tends.

The LORD is good:
  his kindness endures forever,
  and his faithfulness, to all generations.

(From Psalm 100)

Living the Word This Week

How can I make my life a gift for others in charity?

Pray for young people who are discerning a vocation to the priesthood, diaconate, or consecrated life, especially those who will be ordained or make final profession this year.

Thoughts for Today

May 19, 2019

Lectio Divina for the Fifth Week of Easter

We begin our prayer:
In the name of the Father, and of the Son, and of the Holy Spirit.
Amen.

O God, restorer and lover of innocence,
direct the hearts of your servants towards yourself,
that those you have set free from the darkness of unbelief
may never stray from the light of your truth.
Through our Lord Jesus Christ, your Son,
who lives and reigns with you in the unity of the Holy Spirit,
one God, for ever and ever.

(Collect, Wednesday of the Fifth Week of Easter)

Reading (*Lectio*)

Read the following Scripture two or three times.
John 13:31-33a, 34-35

When Judas had left them, Jesus said, "Now is the Son of Man glorified, and God is glorified in him. If God is glorified in him, God will also glorify him in himself, and God will glorify him at once. My children, I will be with you only a little while longer. I give you a new commandment: love one another. As I have loved you, so you also should love one another. This is how all will know that you are my disciples, if you have love for one another."

Meditation (*Meditatio*)

After the reading, take some time to reflect in silence on one or more of the following questions:

- What word or words in this passage caught your attention?
- What in this passage comforted you?
- What in this passage challenged you?

If practicing lectio divina *as a family or in a group, after the reflection time, invite the participants to share their responses.*

Prayer (*Oratio*)

Read the Scripture passage one more time. Bring to the Lord the praise, petition, or thanksgiving that the Word inspires in you.

Contemplation (*Contemplatio*)

Read the Scripture again, followed by this reflection:

What conversion of mind, heart, and life is the Lord asking of me?

Now is the Son of Man glorified, and God is glorified in him. When have I become aware of God's glory? How can I glorify God in my life?

As I have loved you, so you also should love one another. Who has shared God's love with me? With whom do I need to share God's love today?

This is how all will know that you are my disciples. How do people know that I am a disciple of Christ? How can I share my faith more effectively?

After a period of silent reflection and/or discussion, all recite the Lord's Prayer and the following:

Closing Prayer:

The LORD is gracious and merciful,
  slow to anger and of great kindness.
The LORD is good to all
  and compassionate toward all his works.

Let all your works give you thanks, O LORD,
  and let your faithful ones bless you.
Let them discourse of the glory of your kingdom
  and speak of your might.

Let them make known your might to the children of Adam,
  and the glorious splendor of your kingdom.
Your kingdom is a kingdom for all ages,
  and your dominion endures through all generations.

(From Psalm 145)

Living the Word This Week

How can I make my life a gift for others in charity?

Reach out to someone in need: send a note, make a phone call, volunteer some time, make a donation.

Thoughts for Today

May 26, 2019

Lectio Divina for the Sixth Week of Easter

We begin our prayer:
In the name of the Father, and of the Son, and of the Holy Spirit. Amen.

Constantly shape our minds, we pray, O Lord,
by the practice of good works,
that, trying always for what is better,
we may strive to hold ever fast to the Paschal Mystery.
Through our Lord Jesus Christ, your Son,
who lives and reigns with you in the unity of the Holy Spirit,
one God, for ever and ever.

(Collect, Saturday of the Sixth Week of Easter)

Reading (*Lectio*)

Read the following Scripture two or three times.
John 14:23-29

Jesus said to his disciples: "Whoever loves me will keep my word, and my Father will love him, and we will come to him and make our dwelling with him. Whoever does not love me does not keep my words; yet the word you hear is not mine but that of the Father who sent me.

"I have told you this while I am with you. The Advocate, the Holy Spirit, whom the Father will send in my name, will teach you everything and remind you of all that I told you. Peace I leave with you; my peace I give to you. Not as the world gives do I give it to you. Do not let your hearts be troubled or afraid. You heard me tell you, 'I am going away and I will come back to you.' If you loved me, you would rejoice that I am going to the Father; for the Father is greater than I. And now I have told you this before it happens, so that when it happens you may believe."

Meditation (*Meditatio*)

After the reading, take some time to reflect in silence on one or more of the following questions:

- What word or words in this passage caught your attention?
- What in this passage comforted you?
- What in this passage challenged you?

If practicing lectio divina *as a family or in a group, after the reflection time, invite the participants to share their responses.*

Prayer (*Oratio*)

Read the Scripture passage one more time. Bring to the Lord the praise, petition, or thanksgiving that the Word inspires in you.

Contemplation (*Contemplatio*)

Read the Scripture again, followed by this reflection:

What conversion of mind, heart, and life is the Lord asking of me?

Whoever loves me will keep my word. How often do I read or pray with Scripture? How can Scripture help me to discern God's will?

Do not let your hearts be troubled or afraid. What is troubling me? What things calm my heart?

And now I have told you this before it happens, so that when it happens you may believe. What strengthens my faith? How can I support others on their faith journey?

After a period of silent reflection and/or discussion, all recite the Lord's Prayer and the following:

Closing Prayer:

May God have pity on us and bless us;
  may he let his face shine upon us.
So may your way be known upon earth;
  among all nations, your salvation.

May the nations be glad and exult
  because you rule the peoples in equity;
  the nations on the earth you guide.

May the peoples praise you, O God;
  may all the peoples praise you!
May God bless us,
  and may all the ends of the earth fear him!

(From Psalm 67)

Living the Word This Week

How can I make my life a gift for others in charity?

Prepare for Sunday Mass by reading and reflecting on the Scriptures for the day. Use the notes and study aids in your Catholic Bible to come to a better understanding of the Scripture text.

Thoughts for Today

May 30, 2019 or June 2, 2019

Lectio Divina for the Solemnity of the Ascension of the Lord

We begin our prayer:
In the name of the Father, and of the Son, and of the Holy Spirit. Amen.

Gladden us with holy joys, almighty God,
and make us rejoice with devout thanksgiving,
for the Ascension of Christ your Son
is our exaltation,
and, where the Head has gone before in glory,
the Body is called to follow in hope.
Through our Lord Jesus Christ, your Son,
who lives and reigns with you in the unity of the Holy Spirit,
one God, for ever and ever.

(Collect, Ascension, Mass During the Day)

Reading (*Lectio*)

Read the following Scripture two or three times.
Luke 24:46-53

Jesus said to his disciples: "Thus it is written that the Christ would suffer and rise from the dead on the third day and that repentance, for the forgiveness of sins, would be preached in his name to all the nations, beginning from Jerusalem. You are witnesses of these things. And behold I am sending the promise of my Father upon you; but stay in the city until you are clothed with power from on high."

Then he led them out as far as Bethany, raised his hands, and blessed them. As he blessed them he parted from them and was taken up to heaven. They did him homage and then returned to Jerusalem with great joy, and they were continually in the temple praising God.

Meditation (*Meditatio*)

After the reading, take some time to reflect in silence on one or more of the following questions:

- What word or words in this passage caught your attention?
- What in this passage comforted you?
- What in this passage challenged you?

If practicing lectio divina *as a family or in a group, after the reflection time, invite the participants to share their responses.*

Prayer (*Oratio*)

Read the Scripture passage one more time. Bring to the Lord the praise, petition, or thanksgiving that the Word inspires in you.

Contemplation (*Contemplatio*)

Read the Scripture again, followed by this reflection:

What conversion of mind, heart, and life is the Lord asking of me?

Thus it is written that . . . repentance, for the forgiveness of sins, would be preached in his name. For what do I need to repent? How can I open my heart and life to God's mercy and forgiveness?

You are witnesses of these things. Who has witnessed to me about God's saving love? How can I be a better witness to Jesus' mission?

They were continually in the temple praising God. How often do I pray? How can I make more time for prayer and adoration?

After a period of silent reflection and/or discussion, all recite the Lord's Prayer and the following:

Closing Prayer:

All you peoples, clap your hands,
  shout to God with cries of gladness,
For the LORD, the Most High, the awesome,
  is the great king over all the earth.

God mounts his throne amid shouts of joy;
  the LORD, amid trumpet blasts.
Sing praise to God, sing praise;
  sing praise to our king, sing praise.

For king of all the earth is God;
  sing hymns of praise.
God reigns over the nations,
  God sits upon his holy throne.

(From Psalm 47)

Living the Word This Week

How can I make my life a gift for others in charity?

Read the U.S. bishops' pastoral plan for evangelization, *Go and Make Disciples*:

http://www.usccb.org/beliefs-and-teachings/how-we-teach/evangelization/go-and-make-disciples/go-and-make-disciples-a-national-plan-and-strategy-for-catholic-evangelization-in-the-united-states.cfm.

Thoughts for Today

June 2, 2019

Lectio Divina for the Seventh Week of Easter

We begin our prayer:
In the name of the Father, and of the Son, and of the Holy Spirit.
Amen.

May the power of the Holy Spirit
come to us, we pray, O Lord,
that we may keep your will faithfully in mind
and express it in a devout way of life.
Through our Lord Jesus Christ, your Son,
who lives and reigns with you in the unity of the Holy Spirit,
one God, for ever and ever.

(Collect, Monday of the Seventh Week of Easter)

Reading (*Lectio*)

Read the following Scripture two or three times.
John 17:20-26

Lifting up his eyes to heaven, Jesus prayed saying: "Holy Father, I pray not only for them, but also for those who will believe in me through their word, so that they may all be one, as you, Father, are in me and I in you, that they also may be in us, that the world may believe that you sent me. And I have given them the glory you gave me, so that they may be one, as we are one, I in them and you in me, that they may be brought to perfection as one, that the world may know that you sent me, and that you loved them even as you loved me. Father, they are your gift to me. I wish that where I am they also may be with me, that they may see my glory that you gave me, because you loved me before the foundation of the world. Righteous

Father, the world also does not know you, but I know you, and they know that you sent me. I made known to them your name and I will make it known, that the love with which you loved me may be in them and I in them."

Meditation (*Meditatio*)

After the reading, take some time to reflect in silence on one or more of the following questions:

- What word or words in this passage caught your attention?
- What in this passage comforted you?
- What in this passage challenged you?

If practicing lectio divina *as a family or in a group, after the reflection time, invite the participants to share their responses.*

Prayer (*Oratio*)

Read the Scripture passage one more time. Bring to the Lord the praise, petition, or thanksgiving that the Word inspires in you.

Contemplation (*Contemplatio*)

Read the Scripture again, followed by this reflection:

What conversion of mind, heart, and life is the Lord asking of me?

I pray not only for them, but also for those who will believe in me through their word. Whose words helped my faith grow stronger? Who needs my prayers today?

So that they may be one, as we are one. What divisions in my life need to be healed? How can I unite my will to God's will for me?

I made known to them your name and I will make it known, that the love with which you loved me may be in them and I in them. How do I make God's name known? How have I experienced God's love this week?

After a period of silent reflection and/or discussion, all recite the Lord's Prayer and the following:

Closing Prayer:

The LORD is king; let the earth rejoice;
  let the many islands be glad.
Justice and judgment are the foundation of his throne.

The heavens proclaim his justice,
  and all peoples see his glory.
All gods are prostrate before him.

You, O LORD, are the Most High over all the earth,
  exalted far above all gods.

(From Psalm 97)

Living the Word This Week

How can I make my life a gift for others in charity?

Participate in an ecumenical event or dialogue sponsored by your parish or diocese and pray for the unity of all Christians.

Thoughts for Today

June 9, 2019

Lectio Divina for the Solemnity of Pentecost

We begin our prayer:
In the name of the Father, and of the Son, and of the Holy Spirit. Amen.

Grant, we pray, almighty God,
that your Church may always remain that holy people,
formed as one by the unity of Father, Son and Holy Spirit,
which manifests to the world
the Sacrament of your holiness and unity
and leads it to the perfection of your charity.
Through Christ our Lord.

(Collect after the First Reading, Extended Vigil of Pentecost)

Reading (*Lectio*)

Read the following Scripture two or three times.
John 14:15-16, 23b-26

Jesus said to his disciples: "If you love me, you will keep my commandments. And I will ask the Father, and he will give you another Advocate to be with you always.

"Whoever loves me will keep my word, and my Father will love him, and we will come to him and make our dwelling with him. Those who do not love me do not keep my words; yet the word you hear is not mine but that of the Father who sent me.

"I have told you this while I am with you. The Advocate, the Holy Spirit whom the Father will send in my name, will teach you everything and remind you of all that I told you."

Meditation (*Meditatio*)

After the reading, take some time to reflect in silence on one or more of the following questions:

- What word or words in this passage caught your attention?
- What in this passage comforted you?
- What in this passage challenged you?

If practicing lectio divina *as a family or in a group, after the reflection time, invite the participants to share their responses.*

Prayer (*Oratio*)

Read the Scripture passage one more time. Bring to the Lord the praise, petition, or thanksgiving that the Word inspires in you.

Contemplation (*Contemplatio*)

Read the Scripture again, followed by this reflection:

What conversion of mind, heart, and life is the Lord asking of me?

If you love me, you will keep my commandments. How can I express my love for God more intensely? How can I show love for my neighbors, especially those most easily forgotten?

We will come to him and make our dwelling with him. Do I make room in my life for God to take up his dwelling? How often do I rest in the presence of God?

The Advocate, the Holy Spirit whom the Father will send in my name, will teach you everything and remind you of all that I told you. What teachings of the Church would I like to learn more about? How diligent am I about continuing my formation in faith?

After a period of silent reflection and/or discussion, all recite the Lord's Prayer and the following:

Closing Prayer:

Bless the Lord, O my soul!
  O Lord, my God, you are great indeed!
How manifold are your works, O Lord!
  The earth is full of your creatures;

May the glory of the Lord endure forever;
  may the Lord be glad in his works!
Pleasing to him be my theme;
  I will be glad in the Lord.

If you take away their breath, they perish
  and return to their dust.
When you send forth your spirit, they are created,
  and you renew the face of the earth.

(From Psalm 104)

Living the Word This Week

How can I make my life a gift for others in charity?

Pray for those received into the Church this Easter and for all who have received the gift of the Holy Spirit in Confirmation. Ask your pastor about how you can become a sponsor.

Thoughts for Today

June 16, 2019

Lectio Divina for the Solemnity of the Most Holy Trinity

We begin our prayer:
In the name of the Father, and of the Son, and of the Holy Spirit.
Amen.

God our Father, who by sending into the world
the Word of truth and the Spirit of sanctification
made known to the human race your wondrous mystery,
grant us, we pray, that in professing the true faith,
we may acknowledge the Trinity of eternal glory
and adore your Unity, powerful in majesty.
Through our Lord Jesus Christ, your Son,
who lives and reigns with you in the unity of the Holy Spirit,
one God, for ever and ever.

(Collect, Most Holy Trinity)

Reading (*Lectio*)

Read the following Scripture two or three times.
John 16:12-15

Jesus said to his disciples: "I have much more to tell you, but you cannot bear it now. But when he comes, the Spirit of truth, he will guide you to all truth. He will not speak on his own, but he will speak what he hears, and will declare to you the things that are coming. He will glorify me, because he will take from what is mine and declare it to you. Everything that the Father has is mine; for this reason I told you that he will take from what is mine and declare it to you."

Meditation (*Meditatio*)

After the reading, take some time to reflect in silence on one or more of the following questions:

- What word or words in this passage caught your attention?
- What in this passage comforted you?
- What in this passage challenged you?

If practicing lectio divina *as a family or in a group, after the reflection time, invite the participants to share their responses.*

Prayer (*Oratio*)

Read the Scripture passage one more time. Bring to the Lord the praise, petition, or thanksgiving that the Word inspires in you.

Contemplation (*Contemplatio*)

Read the Scripture again, followed by this reflection:

What conversion of mind, heart, and life is the Lord asking of me?

I have much more to tell you, but you cannot bear it now. What burdens do I need to bring to the Lord? How can I help others bear their burdens?

The Spirit of truth, he will guide you to all truth. How can I speak the truth in love? How can I bring greater truth and kindness to my interactions on social media?

He will not speak on his own, but he will speak what he hears. When was the last time I spoke to someone about my faith? How can Scripture and Church teaching help me to form my conscience?

After a period of silent reflection and/or discussion, all recite the Lord's Prayer and the following:

Closing Prayer:

When I behold your heavens, the work of your fingers,
the moon and the stars which you set in place—
What is man that you should be mindful of him,
or the son of man that you should care for him?

You have made him little less than the angels,
and crowned him with glory and honor.
You have given him rule over the works of your hands,
putting all things under his feet:

All sheep and oxen,
yes, and the beasts of the field,
The birds of the air, the fishes of the sea,
and whatever swims the paths of the seas.

(From Psalm 8)

Living the Word This Week

How can I make my life a gift for others in charity?

Read Pope Francis's message on truth in journalism:

http://w2.vatican.va/content/francesco/en/messages/communications/documents/papa-francesco_20180124_messaggio-comunicazioni-sociali.html.

Thoughts for Today

June 23, 2019

Lectio Divina for the Solemnity of the Most Holy Body and Blood of Christ

We begin our prayer:
In the name of the Father, and of the Son, and of the Holy Spirit. Amen.

O God, who in this wonderful Sacrament
have left us a memorial of your Passion,
grant us, we pray,
so to revere the sacred mysteries of your Body and Blood
that we may always experience in ourselves
the fruits of your redemption.
Who live and reign with God the Father
in the unity of the Holy Spirit,
one God, for ever and ever.

(Collect, Most Holy Body and Blood of Christ)

Reading (*Lectio*)

Read the following Scripture two or three times.
Luke 9:11b-17

Jesus spoke to the crowds about the kingdom of God, and he healed those who needed to be cured. As the day was drawing to a close, the Twelve approached him and said, "Dismiss the crowd so that they can go to the surrounding villages and farms and find lodging and provisions; for we are in a deserted place here." He said to them, "Give them some food yourselves." They replied, "Five loaves and two fish are all we have, unless we ourselves go and buy food for all these people." Now the men there numbered about five thousand.

Then he said to his disciples, "Have them sit down in groups of about fifty." They did so and made them all sit down. Then taking the five loaves and the two fish, and looking up to heaven, he said the blessing over them, broke them, and gave them to the disciples to set before the crowd. They all ate and were satisfied. And when the leftover fragments were picked up, they filled twelve wicker baskets.

Meditation (*Meditatio*)

After the reading, take some time to reflect in silence on one or more of the following questions:

- What word or words in this passage caught your attention?
- What in this passage comforted you?
- What in this passage challenged you?

If practicing lectio divina *as a family or in a group, after the reflection time, invite the participants to share their responses.*

Prayer (*Oratio*)

Read the Scripture passage one more time. Bring to the Lord the praise, petition, or thanksgiving that the Word inspires in you.

Contemplation (*Contemplatio*)

Read the Scripture again, followed by this reflection:

What conversion of mind, heart, and life is the Lord asking of me?

He healed those who needed to be cured. From what do I need to be healed? How can I help bring healing to those around me?

Give them some food yourselves. What steps can I take to minimize food waste and share with those who do not have enough? For what do I hunger?

They all ate and were satisfied. In what do I find satisfaction? How can I spend more time enjoying the company of my family and loved ones?

After a period of silent reflection and/or discussion, all recite the Lord's Prayer and the following:

Closing Prayer:

The LORD said to my Lord: "Sit at my right hand
till I make your enemies your footstool."

The scepter of your power the LORD will stretch forth from Zion:
"Rule in the midst of your enemies."

"Yours is princely power in the day of your birth, in holy splendor;
before the daystar, like the dew, I have begotten you."

The LORD has sworn, and he will not repent:
"You are a priest forever, according to the order of
Melchizedek."

(From Psalm 110)

Living the Word This Week

How can I make my life a gift for others in charity?

Spend some time in prayer before the Blessed Sacrament, thanking God for the gift of Christ in the Eucharist.

Thoughts for Today

June 30, 2019

Lectio Divina for the Thirteenth Week in Ordinary Time

We begin our prayer:
In the name of the Father, and of the Son, and of the Holy Spirit. Amen.

O God, who through the grace of adoption
chose us to be children of light,
grant, we pray,
that we may not be wrapped in the darkness of error
but always be seen to stand in the bright light of truth.
Through our Lord Jesus Christ, your Son,
who lives and reigns with you in the unity of the Holy Spirit,
one God, for ever and ever.

(Collect, Thirteenth Sunday in Ordinary Time)

Reading (*Lectio*)

Read the following Scripture two or three times.
Luke 9:51-62

When the days for Jesus' being taken up were fulfilled, he resolutely determined to journey to Jerusalem, and he sent messengers ahead of him. On the way they entered a Samaritan village to prepare for his reception there, but they would not welcome him because the destination of his journey was Jerusalem. When the disciples James and John saw this they asked, "Lord, do you want us to call down fire from heaven to consume them?" Jesus turned and rebuked them, and they journeyed to another village.

As they were proceeding on their journey someone said to him, "I will follow you wherever you go." Jesus answered him, "Foxes have dens and birds of the sky have nests, but the Son of Man has nowhere to rest his head."

And to another he said, "Follow me." But he replied, "Lord, let me go first and bury my father." But he answered him, "Let the dead bury their dead. But you, go and proclaim the kingdom of God." And another said, "I will follow you, Lord, but first let me say farewell to my family at home." To him Jesus said, "No one who sets a hand to the plow and looks to what was left behind is fit for the kingdom of God."

Meditation (*Meditatio*)

After the reading, take some time to reflect in silence on one or more of the following questions:

- What word or words in this passage caught your attention?
- What in this passage comforted you?
- What in this passage challenged you?

If practicing lectio divina *as a family or in a group, after the reflection time, invite the participants to share their responses.*

Prayer (*Oratio*)

Read the Scripture passage one more time. Bring to the Lord the praise, petition, or thanksgiving that the Word inspires in you.

Contemplation (*Contemplatio*)

Read the Scripture again, followed by this reflection:

What conversion of mind, heart, and life is the Lord asking of me?

They would not welcome him. Where have I felt unwelcomed? Who needs my welcome today?

I will follow you wherever you go. To where is Jesus calling me to follow him? Where am I afraid to follow?

No one who sets a hand to the plow and looks to what was left behind is fit for the kingdom of God. What obstacles prevent me from following Jesus? What sins, behaviors, attitudes do I struggle to leave behind?

After a period of silent reflection and/or discussion, all recite the Lord's Prayer and the following:

Closing Prayer:

Keep me, O God, for in you I take refuge;
I say to the LORD, "My Lord are you.
O LORD, my allotted portion and my cup,
you it is who hold fast my lot."

I bless the LORD who counsels me;
even in the night my heart exhorts me.
I set the LORD ever before me;
with him at my right hand I shall not be disturbed.

Therefore my heart is glad and my soul rejoices,
my body, too, abides in confidence
because you will not abandon my soul to the netherworld,
nor will you suffer your faithful one to undergo corruption.

You will show me the path to life,
fullness of joys in your presence,
the delights at your right hand forever.

(From Psalm 16)

Living the Word This Week

How can I make my life a gift for others in charity?

Learn what that Church is doing to protect the life and dignity of migrants and refugees at *www.sharethejourney.org.*

Thoughts for Today

July 7, 2019

Lectio Divina for the Fourteenth Week in Ordinary Time

We begin our prayer:
In the name of the Father, and of the Son, and of the Holy Spirit. Amen.

O God, who in the abasement of your Son
have raised up a fallen world,
fill your faithful with holy joy,
for on those you have rescued from slavery to sin
you bestow eternal gladness.
Through our Lord Jesus Christ, your Son,
who lives and reigns with you in the unity of the Holy Spirit,
one God, for ever and ever.

(Collect, Fourteenth Sunday in Ordinary Time)

Reading (*Lectio*)

Read the following Scripture two or three times.
Luke 10:1-12, 17-20

At that time the Lord appointed seventy-two others whom he sent ahead of him in pairs to every town and place he intended to visit. He said to them, "The harvest is abundant but the laborers are few; so ask the master of the harvest to send out laborers for his harvest. Go on your way; behold, I am sending you like lambs among wolves. Carry no money bag, no sack, no sandals; and greet no one along the way. Into whatever house you enter, first say, 'Peace to this household.' If a peaceful person lives there, your peace will rest on him; but if not, it will return to you. Stay in the same house and eat and drink what is offered to you, for the laborer deserves his payment. Do not move about from one house to another. Whatever town you enter and they welcome you, eat what is set before you, cure the sick in it and say to them, 'The kingdom of God is at hand for you.' Whatever town you enter and they do not receive you, go out into the streets and say, 'The dust of your town that clings to our feet, even that we shake off against you.' Yet know this: the kingdom of God is at hand. I tell you, it will be more tolerable for Sodom on that day than for that town."

The seventy-two returned rejoicing, and said, "Lord, even the demons are subject to us because of your name." Jesus said, "I have observed Satan fall like lightning from the sky. Behold, I have given you the power to 'tread upon serpents' and scorpions and upon the full force of the enemy and nothing will harm you. Nevertheless, do not rejoice because the spirits are subject to you, but rejoice because your names are written in heaven."

Meditation (*Meditatio*)

After the reading, take some time to reflect in silence on one or more of the following questions:

- What word or words in this passage caught your attention?
- What in this passage comforted you?
- What in this passage challenged you?

If practicing lectio divina *as a family or in a group, after the reflection time, invite the participants to share their responses.*

Prayer (*Oratio*)

Read the Scripture passage one more time. Bring to the Lord the praise, petition, or thanksgiving that the Word inspires in you.

Contemplation (*Contemplatio*)

Read the Scripture again, followed by this reflection:

What conversion of mind, heart, and life is the Lord asking of me?

At that time the Lord appointed seventy-two others whom he sent ahead of him in pairs to every town and place he intended to visit. Where do I find Christian community? How can I be a herald of the Lord's coming?

The harvest is abundant but the laborers are few; so ask the master of the harvest to send out laborers for his harvest. How can I support those who are discerning their vocation? How is God calling me to help bring in the harvest?

If a peaceful person lives there, your peace will rest on him. What parts of my life and community lack peace? How can I help bring God's peace to these places?

After a period of silent reflection and/or discussion, all recite the Lord's Prayer and the following:

Closing Prayer:

Shout joyfully to God, all the earth,
  sing praise to the glory of his name;
  proclaim his glorious praise.
Say to God, "How tremendous are your deeds!"

"Let all on earth worship and sing praise to you,
  sing praise to your name!"
Come and see the works of God,
  his tremendous deeds among the children of Adam.

He has changed the sea into dry land;
  through the river they passed on foot;
  therefore let us rejoice in him.
He rules by his might forever.

Hear now, all you who fear God, while I declare
what he has done for me.
Blessed be God who refused me not
my prayer or his kindness!

(From Psalm 66)

Living the Word This Week

How can I make my life a gift for others in charity?

Research ways to support vocation discernment in your diocese through prayer and action.

Thoughts for Today

July 14, 2019

Lectio Divina for the Fifteenth Week in Ordinary Time

We begin our prayer:
In the name of the Father, and of the Son, and of the Holy Spirit.
Amen.

O God, who show the light of your truth
to those who go astray,
so that they may return to the right path,
give all who for the faith they profess
are accounted Christians
the grace to reject whatever is contrary to the name of Christ
and to strive after all that does it honor.
Through our Lord Jesus Christ, your Son,
who lives and reigns with you in the unity of the Holy Spirit,
one God, for ever and ever.

(Collect, Fifteenth Sunday in Ordinary Time)

Reading (*Lectio*)

Read the following Scripture two or three times.
Luke 10:25-37

There was a scholar of the law who stood up to test him and said, "Teacher, what must I do to inherit eternal life?" Jesus said to him, "What is written in the law? How do you read it?" He said in reply, *You shall love the Lord, your God, with all your heart, with all your being, with all your strength, and with all your mind, and your neighbor as yourself.*" He replied to him, "You have answered correctly; do this and you will live."

But because he wished to justify himself, he said to Jesus, "And who is my neighbor?" Jesus replied, "A man fell victim to robbers as he went down from Jerusalem to Jericho. They stripped and beat him and went off leaving him half-dead. A priest happened to be going down that road, but when he saw him, he passed by on the opposite side. Likewise a Levite came to the place, and when he saw him, he passed by on the opposite side. But a Samaritan traveler who came upon him was moved with compassion at the sight. He approached the victim, poured oil and wine over his wounds and bandaged them. Then he lifted him up on his own animal, took him to an inn, and cared for him. The next day he took out two silver coins and gave them to the innkeeper with the instruction, 'Take care of him. If you spend more than what I have given you, I shall repay you on my way back.' Which of these three, in your opinion, was neighbor to the robbers' victim?" He answered, "The one who treated him with mercy." Jesus said to him, "Go and do likewise."

Meditation (*Meditatio*)

After the reading, take some time to reflect in silence on one or more of the following questions:

- What word or words in this passage caught your attention?
- What in this passage comforted you?
- What in this passage challenged you?

If practicing lectio divina *as a family or in a group, after the reflection time, invite the participants to share their responses.*

Prayer (*Oratio*)

Read the Scripture passage one more time. Bring to the Lord the praise, petition, or thanksgiving that the Word inspires in you.

Contemplation (*Contemplatio*)

Read the Scripture again, followed by this reflection:

What conversion of mind, heart, and life is the Lord asking of me?

But because he wished to justify himself, he said to Jesus, "And who is my neighbor?" Who is my neighbor? What neighbors do I not see?

But a Samaritan traveler who came upon him was moved with compassion at the sight. What moves me with compassion? Against what needs have I hardened my heart?

"Which of these three, in your opinion, was neighbor to the robbers' victim?" He answered, "The one who treated him with mercy." Jesus said to him, "Go and do likewise." What does it mean to treat someone with mercy? How can I be more merciful?

After a period of silent reflection and/or discussion, all recite the Lord's Prayer and the following:

Closing Prayer:

I pray to you, O LORD,
  for the time of your favor, O God!
In your great kindness answer me
  with your constant help.
Answer me, O LORD, for bounteous is your kindness:
  in your great mercy turn toward me.

I am afflicted and in pain;
  let your saving help, O God, protect me.
I will praise the name of God in song,
  and I will glorify him with thanksgiving.

"See, you lowly ones, and be glad;
  you who seek God, may your hearts revive!
For the LORD hears the poor,
  and his own who are in bonds he spurns not."

For God will save Zion
  and rebuild the cities of Judah.
The descendants of his servants shall inherit it,
  and those who love his name shall inhabit it.

(From Psalm 69)

Living the Word This Week

How can I make my life a gift for others in charity?

Find a way to participate in your parish or diocesan ministries of charity and social justice through advocacy, service, prayer, or financial support.

Thoughts for Today

July 21, 2019

Lectio Divina for the Sixteenth Week in Ordinary Time

We begin our prayer:
In the name of the Father, and of the Son, and of the Holy Spirit.
Amen.

Show favor, O Lord, to your servants
and mercifully increase the gifts of your grace,
that, made fervent in hope, faith and charity,
they may be ever watchful in keeping your commands.
Through our Lord Jesus Christ, your Son,
who lives and reigns with you in the unity of the Holy Spirit,
one God, for ever and ever.

(Collect, Sixteenth Sunday in Ordinary Time)

Reading (*Lectio*)

Read the following Scripture two or three times.
Luke 10:38-42

Jesus entered a village where a woman whose name was Martha welcomed him. She had a sister named Mary who sat beside the Lord at his feet listening to him speak. Martha, burdened with much serving, came to him and said, "Lord, do you not care that my sister has left me by myself to do the serving? Tell her to help me." The Lord said to her in reply, "Martha, Martha, you are anxious and worried about many things. There is need of only one thing. Mary has chosen the better part and it will not be taken from her."

Meditation (*Meditatio*)

After the reading, take some time to reflect in silence on one or more of the following questions:

- What word or words in this passage caught your attention?
- What in this passage comforted you?
- What in this passage challenged you?

If practicing lectio divina *as a family or in a group, after the reflection time, invite the participants to share their responses.*

Prayer (*Oratio*)

Read the Scripture passage one more time. Bring to the Lord the praise, petition, or thanksgiving that the Word inspires in you.

Contemplation (*Contemplatio*)

Read the Scripture again, followed by this reflection:

What conversion of mind, heart, and life is the Lord asking of me?

A woman whose name was Martha welcomed him. Who do I need to welcome into my community? My home? My life? How can I express this welcome?

You are anxious and worried about many things. About what am I anxious or worried? What support or assistance do I need to address these concerns?

There is need of only one thing. What needs do I feel in the depths of my heart? What needs of others can I help to meet?

After a period of silent reflection and/or discussion, all recite the Lord's Prayer and the following:

Closing Prayer:

One who walks blamelessly and does justice;
who thinks the truth in his heart
and slanders not with his tongue.

Who harms not his fellow man,
    nor takes up a reproach against his neighbor;
by whom the reprobate is despised,
    while he honors those who fear the LORD.

Who lends not his money at usury
    and accepts no bribe against the innocent.
One who does these things
    shall never be disturbed.

(From Psalm 15)

Living the Word This Week

How can I make my life a gift for others in charity?

Volunteer to assist your parish in welcoming new parishioners or those visiting the parish.

Thoughts for Today

July 28, 2019

Lectio Divina for the Seventeenth Week in Ordinary Time

We begin our prayer:
In the name of the Father, and of the Son, and of the Holy Spirit. Amen.

O God, protector of those who hope in you,
without whom nothing has firm foundation, nothing is holy,
bestow in abundance your mercy upon us
and grant that, with you as our ruler and guide,
we may use the good things that pass
in such a way as to hold fast even now
to those that ever endure.
Through our Lord Jesus Christ, your Son,
who lives and reigns with you in the unity of the Holy Spirit,
one God, for ever and ever.

(Collect, Seventeenth Sunday in Ordinary Time)

Reading (*Lectio*)

Read the following Scripture two or three times.
Luke 11:1-13

Jesus was praying in a certain place, and when he had finished, one of his disciples said to him, "Lord, teach us to pray just as John taught his disciples." He said to them, "When you pray, say:

Father, hallowed be your name,
  your kingdom come.
  Give us each day our daily bread

and forgive us our sins
for we ourselves forgive everyone in debt to us,
and do not subject us to the final test."

And he said to them, "Suppose one of you has a friend to whom he goes at midnight and says, 'Friend, lend me three loaves of bread, for a friend of mine has arrived at my house from a journey and I have nothing to offer him,' and he says in reply from within, 'Do not bother me; the door has already been locked and my children and I are already in bed. I cannot get up to give you anything.' I tell you, if he does not get up to give the visitor the loaves because of their friendship, he will get up to give him whatever he needs because of his persistence.

"And I tell you, ask and you will receive; seek and you will find; knock and the door will be opened to you. For everyone who asks, receives; and the one who seeks, finds; and to the one who knocks, the door will be opened. What father among you would hand his son a snake when he asks for a fish? Or hand him a scorpion when he asks for an egg? If you then, who are wicked, know how to give good gifts to your children, how much more will the Father in heaven give the Holy Spirit to those who ask him?"

Meditation (*Meditatio*)

After the reading, take some time to reflect in silence on one or more of the following questions:

- What word or words in this passage caught your attention?
- What in this passage comforted you?
- What in this passage challenged you?

If practicing lectio divina *as a family or in a group, after the reflection time, invite the participants to share their responses.*

Prayer (*Oratio*)

Read the Scripture passage one more time. Bring to the Lord the praise, petition, or thanksgiving that the Word inspires in you.

Contemplation (*Contemplatio*)

Read the Scripture again, followed by this reflection:

What conversion of mind, heart, and life is the Lord asking of me?

Lord, teach us to pray. What types of prayer nurture my soul? When and where do I pray most intently?

Forgive us our sins / for we ourselves forgive everyone in debt to us. Who do I need to forgive? From whom do I need to ask forgiveness?

If you then, who are wicked, know how to give good gifts to your children, how much more will the Father in heaven give the Holy Spirit to those who ask him? For what gifts do I need to ask God? How can I be more generous in giving to others?

After a period of silent reflection and/or discussion, all recite the Lord's Prayer and the following:

Closing Prayer:

I will give thanks to you, O Lord, with all my heart,
  for you have heard the words of my mouth;
  in the presence of the angels I will sing your praise;
I will worship at your holy temple
  and give thanks to your name.

Because of your kindness and your truth;
  for you have made great above all things
  your name and your promise.
When I called you answered me;
  you built up strength within me.

The Lord is exalted, yet the lowly he sees,
  and the proud he knows from afar.

Though I walk amid distress, you preserve me;
against the anger of my enemies you raise your hand.

Your right hand saves me.
The LORD will complete what he has done for me;
your kindness, O LORD, endures forever;
forsake not the work of your hands.

(From Psalm 138)

Living the Word This Week

How can I make my life a gift for others in charity?

Schedule time on your calendar to pray each day this week. Consider varying the type of prayer each day: the Liturgy of the Hours, the Rosary, Eucharistic adoration, contemplative prayer, etc.

Thoughts for Today

August 4, 2019

Lectio Divina for the Eighteenth Week in Ordinary Time

We begin our prayer:
In the name of the Father, and of the Son, and of the Holy Spirit. Amen.

Draw near to your servants, O Lord,
and answer their prayers with unceasing kindness,
that, for those who glory in you as their Creator and guide,
you may restore what you have created
and keep safe what you have restored.
Through our Lord Jesus Christ, your Son,
who lives and reigns with you in the unity of the Holy Spirit,
one God, for ever and ever.

(Collect, Eighteenth Sunday in Ordinary Time)

Reading (*Lectio*)

Read the following Scripture two or three times.
Luke 12:13-21

Someone in the crowd said to Jesus, "Teacher, tell my brother to share the inheritance with me." He replied to him, "Friend, who appointed me as your judge and arbitrator?" Then he said to the crowd, "Take care to guard against all greed, for though one may be rich, one's life does not consist of possessions."

Then he told them a parable. "There was a rich man whose land produced a bountiful harvest. He asked himself, 'What shall I do, for I do not have space to store my harvest?' And he said, 'This is what I shall do: I shall tear down my barns and build larger ones. There I shall store all my grain and other goods and I shall say to myself, "Now as for you, you have so many good things stored up for many years, rest, eat, drink, be merry!"' But God said to him, 'You fool, this night your life will be demanded of you; and the things you have prepared, to whom will they belong?' Thus will it be for all who store up treasure for themselves but are not rich in what matters to God."

Meditation (*Meditatio*)

After the reading, take some time to reflect in silence on one or more of the following questions:

- What word or words in this passage caught your attention?
- What in this passage comforted you?
- What in this passage challenged you?

If practicing lectio divina *as a family or in a group, after the reflection time, invite the participants to share their responses.*

Prayer (*Oratio*)

Read the Scripture passage one more time. Bring to the Lord the praise, petition, or thanksgiving that the Word inspires in you.

Contemplation (*Contemplatio*)

Read the Scripture again, followed by this reflection:

What conversion of mind, heart, and life is the Lord asking of me?

Teacher, tell my brother to share the inheritance with me. What gifts am I called to share with my brothers and sisters? What do I expect my brothers and sisters to share with me?

One's life does not consist of possessions. What things do I most value in my life? How does my use of time and money reflect those values?

Thus will it be for all who store up treasure for themselves but are not rich in what matters to God. What matters to God? How can I re-orient my life to focus on those things?

After a period of silent reflection and/or discussion, all recite the Lord's Prayer and the following:

Closing Prayer:

You turn man back to dust,
    saying, "Return, O children of men."
For a thousand years in your sight
    are as yesterday, now that it is past,
    or as a watch of the night.

You make an end of them in their sleep;
    the next morning they are like the changing grass,
Which at dawn springs up anew,
    but by evening wilts and fades.

Teach us to number our days aright,
    that we may gain wisdom of heart.
Return, O LORD! How long?
    Have pity on your servants!

Fill us at daybreak with your kindness,
    that we may shout for joy and gladness all our days.
And may the gracious care of the LORD our God be ours;
    prosper the work of our hands for us!
    Prosper the work of our hands!

(From Psalm 90)

Living the Word This Week

How can I make my life a gift for others in charity?

Re-examine how you use your time, treasure, and talent to ensure that you are using them in support of what you value most.

Thoughts for Today

August 11, 2019

Lectio Divina for the Nineteenth Week in Ordinary Time

We begin our prayer:
In the name of the Father, and of the Son, and of the Holy Spirit. Amen.

Almighty ever-living God,
whom, taught by the Holy Spirit,
we dare to call our Father,
bring, we pray, to perfection in our hearts
the spirit of adoption as your sons and daughters,
that we may merit to enter into the inheritance
which you have promised.
Through our Lord Jesus Christ, your Son,
who lives and reigns with you in the unity of the Holy Spirit,
one God, for ever and ever.

(Collect, Nineteenth Sunday in Ordinary Time)

Reading (*Lectio*)

Read the following Scripture two or three times.
Luke 12:32-48

Jesus said to his disciples: "Do not be afraid any longer, little flock, for your Father is pleased to give you the kingdom. Sell your belongings and give alms. Provide money bags for yourselves that do not wear out, an inexhaustible treasure in heaven that no thief can reach nor moth destroy. For where your treasure is, there also will your heart be.

"Gird your loins and light your lamps and be like servants who await their master's return from a wedding, ready to open immediately when he comes and knocks. Blessed are those servants whom the master finds vigilant on his arrival. Amen, I say to you, he will gird himself, have them recline at table, and proceed to wait on them. And should he come in the second or third watch and find them prepared in this way, blessed are those servants. Be sure of this: if the master of the house had known the hour when the thief was coming, he would not have let his house be broken into. You also must be prepared, for at an hour you do not expect, the Son of Man will come."

Then Peter said, "Lord, is this parable meant for us or for everyone?" And the Lord replied, "Who, then, is the faithful and prudent steward whom the master will put in charge of his servants to distribute the food allowance at the proper time? Blessed is that servant whom his master on arrival finds doing so. Truly, I say to you, the master will put the servant in charge of all his property. But if that servant says to himself, 'My master is delayed in coming,' and begins to beat the menservants and the maidservants, to eat and drink and get drunk, then that servant's master will come on an unexpected day and at an unknown hour and will punish the servant severely and assign him a place with the unfaithful. That servant who knew his master's will but did not make preparations nor act in accord with his will shall be beaten severely; and the servant who was ignorant of his master's will but acted in a way deserving of a severe beating shall be beaten only lightly. Much will be required of the person entrusted with much, and still more will be demanded of the person entrusted with more."

Meditation (*Meditatio*)

After the reading, take some time to reflect in silence on one or more of the following questions:

- What word or words in this passage caught your attention?
- What in this passage comforted you?
- What in this passage challenged you?

If practicing lectio divina *as a family or in a group, after the reflection time, invite the participants to share their responses.*

Prayer (*Oratio*)

Read the Scripture passage one more time. Bring to the Lord the praise, petition, or thanksgiving that the Word inspires in you.

Contemplation (*Contemplatio*)

Read the Scripture again, followed by this reflection:

What conversion of mind, heart, and life is the Lord asking of me?

Do not be afraid any longer, little flock, for your Father is pleased to give you the kingdom. How does my hope in God's kingdom dispel my fear? How can I help to build God's kingdom?

You also must be prepared, for at an hour you do not expect, the Son of Man will come. How am I preparing for Jesus' return? How is God part of my vision for my future?

Much will be required of the person entrusted with much, and still more will be demanded of the person entrusted with more. With what gifts has God entrusted me? How can I use these gifts to build God's kingdom?

After a period of silent reflection and/or discussion, all recite the Lord's Prayer and the following:

Closing Prayer:

Exult, you just, in the LORD;
praise from the upright is fitting.
Blessed the nation whose God is the LORD,
the people he has chosen for his own inheritance.

See, the eyes of the LORD are upon those who fear him,
upon those who hope for his kindness,

To deliver them from death
and preserve them in spite of famine.

Our soul waits for the LORD,
who is our help and our shield.
May your kindness, O LORD, be upon us
who have put our hope in you.

(From Psalm 33)

Living the Word This Week

How can I make my life a gift for others in charity?

Explore ways to place your gifts at the service of the Church and of those in need.

Thoughts for Today

August 15, 2019

Lectio Divina for the Solemnity of the Assumption

We begin our prayer:
In the name of the Father, and of the Son, and of the Holy Spirit.
Amen.

Almighty ever-living God,
who assumed the Immaculate Virgin Mary, the Mother of your Son,
body and soul into heavenly glory,
grant, we pray,
that, always attentive to the things that are above,
we may merit to be sharers of her glory.
Through our Lord Jesus Christ, your Son,
who lives and reigns with you in the unity of the Holy Spirit,
one God, for ever and ever.

(Collect, Solemnity of the Assumption)

Reading (*Lectio*)

Read the following Scripture two or three times.
Luke 1:39-56

Mary set out and traveled to the hill country in haste to a town of Judah, where she entered the house of Zechariah and greeted Elizabeth. When Elizabeth heard Mary's greeting, the infant leaped in her womb, and Elizabeth, filled with the Holy Spirit, cried out in a loud voice and said, "Blessed are you among women, and blessed is the fruit of your womb. And how does this happen to me, that the mother of my Lord should come to me? For at the moment the sound of your greeting reached my ears, the infant in my womb leaped for joy. Blessed are you who believed that what was spoken to you by the Lord would be fulfilled."

And Mary said:

"My soul proclaims the greatness of the Lord;
my spirit rejoices in God my Savior
for he has looked with favor on his lowly servant.
From this day all generations will call me blessed:
the Almighty has done great things for me
and holy is his Name.
He has mercy on those who fear him
in every generation.
He has shown the strength of his arm,
and has scattered the proud in their conceit.
He has cast down the mighty from their thrones,
and has lifted up the lowly.
He has filled the hungry with good things,
and the rich he has sent away empty.
He has come to the help of his servant Israel
for he has remembered his promise of mercy,
the promise he made to our fathers,
to Abraham and his children forever."

Mary remained with her about three months and then returned to her home.

Meditation (*Meditatio*)

After the reading, take some time to reflect in silence on one or more of the following questions:

- What word or words in this passage caught your attention?
- What in this passage comforted you?
- What in this passage challenged you?

If practicing lectio divina *as a family or in a group, after the reflection time, invite the participants to share their responses.*

Prayer (*Oratio*)

Read the Scripture passage one more time. Bring to the Lord the praise, petition, or thanksgiving that the Word inspires in you.

Contemplation (*Contemplatio*)

Read the Scripture again, followed by this reflection:

What conversion of mind, heart, and life is the Lord asking of me?

For at the moment the sound of your greeting reached my ears, the infant in my womb leaped for joy. What has brought me joy this week? How can I be a bearer of joy instead of criticism?

Blessed are you who believed that what was spoken to you by the Lord would be fulfilled. What words of the Lord do I struggle to believe? What steps can I take to strengthen my faith?

For he has looked with favor on his lowly servant. How has God shown favor to me? How can I see others with God's caring eyes?

After a period of silent reflection and/or discussion, all recite the Lord's Prayer and the following:

Closing Prayer:

The queen takes her place at your right hand in gold of Ophir.

Hear, O daughter, and see; turn your ear,
forget your people and your father's house.

So shall the king desire your beauty;
for he is your lord.

They are borne in with gladness and joy;
they enter the palace of the king.

(From Psalm 45)

Living the Word This Week

How can I make my life a gift for others in charity?

Donate to or volunteer at a food bank or soup kitchen to help ensure that the hungry are filled with good things.

Thoughts for Today

August 18, 2019

Lectio Divina for the Twentieth Week in Ordinary Time

We begin our prayer:
In the name of the Father, and of the Son, and of the Holy Spirit.
Amen.

O God, who have prepared for those who love you
good things which no eye can see,
fill our hearts, we pray, with the warmth of your love,
so that, loving you in all things and above all things,
we may attain your promises,
which surpass every human desire.
Through our Lord Jesus Christ, your Son,
who lives and reigns with you in the unity of the Holy Spirit,
one God, for ever and ever.

(Collect, Twentieth Sunday in Ordinary Time)

Reading (*Lectio*)

Read the following Scripture two or three times.
Luke 12:49-53

Jesus said to his disciples: "I have come to set the earth on fire, and how I wish it were already blazing! There is a baptism with which I must be baptized, and how great is my anguish until it is accomplished! Do you think that I have come to establish peace on the earth? No, I tell you, but rather division. From now on a household of five will be divided, three against two and two against three; a father will be divided against his son and a son against his father, a mother against her daughter and a daughter against her mother, a mother-in-law against her daughter-in-law and a daughter-in-law against her mother-in-law."

Meditation (*Meditatio*)

After the reading, take some time to reflect in silence on one or more of the following questions:

- What word or words in this passage caught your attention?
- What in this passage comforted you?
- What in this passage challenged you?

If practicing lectio divina *as a family or in a group, after the reflection time, invite the participants to share their responses.*

Prayer (*Oratio*)

Read the Scripture passage one more time. Bring to the Lord the praise, petition, or thanksgiving that the Word inspires in you.

Contemplation (*Contemplatio*)

Read the Scripture again, followed by this reflection:

What conversion of mind, heart, and life is the Lord asking of me?

I have come to set the earth on fire, and how I wish it were already blazing! What in my life needs to be purified by the Lord's healing fire? How can I share the light of Christ and the fire of the Spirit with those I encounter?

There is a baptism with which I must be baptized. To what does my baptismal commitment call me? What challenges do I face in living my baptismal call?

Do you think that I have come to establish peace on the earth? No, I tell you, but rather division. From what worldly values and practices must I separate myself? How can I stand for the truth of God's Word with integrity and love?

After a period of silent reflection and/or discussion, all recite the Lord's Prayer and the following:

Closing Prayer:

I have waited, waited for the LORD,
  and he stooped toward me.

The LORD heard my cry.
He drew me out of the pit of destruction,
  out of the mud of the swamp;
he set my feet upon a crag;
  he made firm my steps.

And he put a new song into my mouth,
  a hymn to our God.
Many shall look on in awe
  and trust in the LORD.

Though I am afflicted and poor,
  yet the LORD thinks of me.
You are my help and my deliverer;
  O my God, hold not back!

(From Psalm 40)

Living the Word This Week

How can I make my life a gift for others in charity?

Get involved with the advocacy efforts sponsored by your diocese or state Catholic conference.

Thoughts for Today

August 25, 2019

Lectio Divina for the Twenty-First Week in Ordinary Time

We begin our prayer:
In the name of the Father, and of the Son, and of the Holy Spirit. Amen.

O God, who cause the minds of the faithful
to unite in a single purpose,
grant your people to love what you command
and to desire what you promise,
that, amid the uncertainties of this world,
our hearts may be fixed on that place
where true gladness is found.
Through our Lord Jesus Christ, your Son,
who lives and reigns with you in the unity of the Holy Spirit,
one God, for ever and ever.

(Collect, Twenty-First Sunday in Ordinary Time)

Reading (*Lectio*)

Read the following Scripture two or three times.
Luke 13:22-30

Jesus passed through towns and villages, teaching as he went and making his way to Jerusalem. Someone asked him, "Lord, will only a few people be saved?" He answered them, "Strive to enter through the narrow gate, for many, I tell you, will attempt to enter but will not be strong enough. After the master of the house has arisen and locked the door, then will you stand outside knocking and saying, 'Lord, open the door for us.' He will say to you in reply, 'I do not know where you are from. And you will say, 'We ate and drank in your company and you taught in our streets.' Then he will say to you, 'I do not know where you are from. Depart from me, all you evildoers!' And there will be wailing and grinding of teeth when you see Abraham, Isaac, and Jacob and all the prophets in the kingdom of God and you yourselves cast out. And people will come from the east and the west and from the north and the south and will recline at table in the kingdom of God. For behold, some are last who will be first, and some are first who will be last."

Meditation (*Meditatio*)

After the reading, take some time to reflect in silence on one or more of the following questions:

- What word or words in this passage caught your attention?
- What in this passage comforted you?
- What in this passage challenged you?

If practicing lectio divina *as a family or in a group, after the reflection time, invite the participants to share their responses.*

Prayer (*Oratio*)

Read the Scripture passage one more time. Bring to the Lord the praise, petition, or thanksgiving that the Word inspires in you.

Contemplation (*Contemplatio*)

Read the Scripture again, followed by this reflection:

What conversion of mind, heart, and life is the Lord asking of me?

Strive to enter through the narrow gate, for many, I tell you, will attempt to enter but will not be strong enough. What things keep me from entering through the narrow gate and living according to God's will? How can I strengthen my faith and my commitment to living according to God's will?

Lord, open the door for us. What doors do I need the Lord to open for me? How can I help other people find and pass through the doors the Lord has opened?

For behold, some are last who will be first, and some are first who will be last. How attentive am I to those that society views as "last"? How can I put forward the interests of those who are last?

After a period of silent reflection and/or discussion, all recite the Lord's Prayer and the following:

Closing Prayer:

Praise the LORD all you nations;
glorify him, all you peoples!

For steadfast is his kindness toward us,
and the fidelity of the LORD endures forever.

(From Psalm 117)

Living the Word This Week

How can I make my life a gift for others in charity?
Invite someone to attend Mass or to pray with you.

Thoughts for Today

September 1, 2019

Lectio Divina for the Twenty-Second Week in Ordinary Time

We begin our prayer:
In the name of the Father, and of the Son, and of the Holy Spirit. Amen.

God of might, giver of every good gift,
put into our hearts the love of your name,
so that, by deepening our sense of reverence,
you may nurture in us what is good
and, by your watchful care,
keep safe what you have nurtured.
Through our Lord Jesus Christ, your Son,
who lives and reigns with you in the unity of the Holy Spirit,
one God, for ever and ever.

(Collect, Twenty-Second Sunday in Ordinary Time)

Reading (*Lectio*)

Read the following Scripture two or three times.
Luke 14:1, 7-14

On a sabbath Jesus went to dine at the home of one of the leading Pharisees, and the people there were observing him carefully.

He told a parable to those who had been invited, noticing how they were choosing the places of honor at the table. "When you are invited by someone to a wedding banquet, do not recline at table in the place of honor. A more distinguished guest than you may have been invited by him, and the host who invited both of you may approach you and say, 'Give your place to this man,' and then you would proceed with embarrassment to take the lowest place. Rather, when you are invited, go and take the lowest place so that when the host comes to you he may say, 'My friend, move up to a higher position.' Then you will enjoy the esteem of your companions at the table. For everyone who exalts himself will be humbled, but the one who humbles himself will be exalted." Then he said to the host who invited him, "When you hold a lunch or a dinner, do not invite your friends or your brothers or your relatives or your wealthy neighbors, in case they may invite you back and you have repayment. Rather, when you hold a banquet, invite the poor, the crippled, the lame, the blind; blessed indeed will you be because of their inability to repay you.

For you will be repaid at the resurrection of the righteous."

Meditation (*Meditatio*)

After the reading, take some time to reflect in silence on one or more of the following questions:

- What word or words in this passage caught your attention?
- What in this passage comforted you?
- What in this passage challenged you?

If practicing lectio divina *as a family or in a group, after the reflection time, invite the participants to share their responses.*

Prayer (*Oratio*)

Read the Scripture passage one more time. Bring to the Lord the praise, petition, or thanksgiving that the Word inspires in you.

Contemplation (*Contemplatio*)

Read the Scripture again, followed by this reflection:

What conversion of mind, heart, and life is the Lord asking of me?

The people there were observing him carefully. Who do I observe to learn how to behave? How can I provide a good example to those who watch me?

For everyone who exalts himself will be humbled, but the one who humbles himself will be exalted. When have I sought the praise of others? How can I make sure that I do good things for the right reasons?

Rather, when you hold a banquet, invite the poor, the crippled, the lame, the blind; blessed indeed will you be because of their inability to repay you. Who is on the peripheries of my life? How can I reach out to these people in love?

After a period of silent reflection and/or discussion, all recite the Lord's Prayer and the following:

Closing Prayer:

The just rejoice and exult before God;
 they are glad and rejoice.
Sing to God, chant praise to his name;
 whose name is the LORD.

The father of orphans and the defender of widows
 is God in his holy dwelling.
God gives a home to the forsaken;
 he leads forth prisoners to prosperity.

A bountiful rain you showered down, O God, upon your inheritance;
 you restored the land when it languished;
your flock settled in it;
 in your goodness, O God, you provided it for the needy.

(From Psalm 68)

Living the Word This Week

How can I make my life a gift for others in charity?

Learn more about the Church's option for the poor and vulnerable:

http://www.usccb.org/beliefs-and-teachings/what-we-believe/catholic-social-teaching/option-for-the-poor-and-vulnerable.cfm.

Thoughts for Today

September 8, 2019

Lectio Divina for the Twenty-Third Week in Ordinary Time

We begin our prayer:
In the name of the Father, and of the Son, and of the Holy Spirit.
Amen.

O God, by whom we are redeemed and receive adoption,
look graciously upon your beloved sons and daughters,
that those who believe in Christ
may receive true freedom
and an everlasting inheritance.
Through our Lord Jesus Christ, your Son,
who lives and reigns with you in the unity of the Holy Spirit,
one God, for ever and ever.

(Collect, Twenty-Third Sunday in Ordinary Time)

Reading (*Lectio*)

Read the following Scripture two or three times.
Luke 14:25-33

Great crowds were traveling with Jesus, and he turned and addressed them, "If anyone comes to me without hating his father and mother, wife and children, brothers and sisters, and even his own life, he cannot be my disciple. Whoever does not carry his own cross and come after me cannot be my disciple. Which of you wishing to construct a tower does not first sit down and calculate the cost to see if there is enough for its completion? Otherwise, after laying the foundation and finding himself unable to finish the work the onlookers should laugh at him and say, 'This one began to build but did not have the resources to finish.' Or what king marching into battle would not first sit down and decide whether with ten thousand troops he can successfully oppose another king advancing upon him with twenty thousand troops? But if not, while he is still far away, he will send a delegation to ask for peace terms. In the same way, anyone of you who does not renounce all his possessions cannot be my disciple."

Meditation (*Meditatio*)

After the reading, take some time to reflect in silence on one or more of the following questions:

- What word or words in this passage caught your attention?
- What in this passage comforted you?
- What in this passage challenged you?

If practicing lectio divina *as a family or in a group, after the reflection time, invite the participants to share their responses.*

Prayer (*Oratio*)

Read the Scripture passage one more time. Bring to the Lord the praise, petition, or thanksgiving that the Word inspires in you.

Contemplation (*Contemplatio*)

Read the Scripture again, followed by this reflection:

What conversion of mind, heart, and life is the Lord asking of me?

Whoever does not carry his own cross and come after me cannot be my disciple. What cross is God asking me to carry? How can I help someone close to me carry her cross?

This one began to build but did not have the resources to finish. What spiritual efforts have I left unfinished? What resources will help me grow in faith, hope, and love?

Anyone of you who does not renounce all his possessions cannot be my disciple. What worldly things or habits distance me from God and my neighbor? What steps can I take to ensure that my possessions do not possess me?

After a period of silent reflection and/or discussion, all recite the Lord's Prayer and the following:

Closing Prayer:

You turn man back to dust,
  saying, "Return, O children of men."
For a thousand years in your sight
  are as yesterday, now that it is past,
  or as a watch of the night.

You make an end of them in their sleep;
  the next morning they are like the changing grass,
Which at dawn springs up anew,
  but by evening wilts and fades.

Teach us to number our days aright,
  that we may gain wisdom of heart.
Return, O LORD! How long?
  Have pity on your servants!

Fill us at daybreak with your kindness,
  that we may shout for joy and gladness all our days.
And may the gracious care of the LORD our God be ours;
  prosper the work of our hands for us!
  Prosper the work of our hands!

(From Psalm 90)

Living the Word This Week

How can I make my life a gift for others in charity?

Learn about and advocate for Christians in other countries who share the cross of Christ by being persecuted for their faith.

Thoughts for Today

September 15, 2019

Lectio Divina for the Twenty-Fourth Week in Ordinary Time

We begin our prayer:
In the name of the Father, and of the Son, and of the Holy Spirit. Amen.

Look upon us, O God,
Creator and ruler of all things,
and, that we may feel the working of your mercy,
grant that we may serve you with all our heart.
Through our Lord Jesus Christ, your Son,
who lives and reigns with you in the unity of the Holy Spirit,
one God, for ever and ever.

(Collect, Twenty-Fourth Sunday in Ordinary Time)

Reading (*Lectio*)

Read the following Scripture two or three times.
Luke 15:1-10

Tax collectors and sinners were all drawing near to listen to Jesus, but the Pharisees and scribes began to complain, saying, "This man welcomes sinners and eats with them." So to them he addressed this parable. "What man among you having a hundred sheep and losing one of them would not leave the ninety-nine in the desert and go after the lost one until he finds it? And when he does find it, he sets it on his shoulders with great joy and, upon his arrival home, he calls together his friends and neighbors and says to them, 'Rejoice with me because I have found my lost sheep.' I tell you, in just the same way there will be more joy in heaven over one sinner who repents than over ninety-nine righteous people who have no need of repentance.

"Or what woman having ten coins and losing one would not light a lamp and sweep the house, searching carefully until she finds it? And when she does find it, she calls together her friends and neighbors and says to them, 'Rejoice with me because I have found the coin that I lost.' In just the same way, I tell you, there will be rejoicing among the angels of God over one sinner who repents."

Meditation (*Meditatio*)

After the reading, take some time to reflect in silence on one or more of the following questions:

- What word or words in this passage caught your attention?
- What in this passage comforted you?
- What in this passage challenged you?

If practicing lectio divina *as a family or in a group, after the reflection time, invite the participants to share their responses.*

Prayer (*Oratio*)

Read the Scripture passage one more time. Bring to the Lord the praise, petition, or thanksgiving that the Word inspires in you.

Contemplation (*Contemplatio*)

Read the Scripture again, followed by this reflection:

What conversion of mind, heart, and life is the Lord asking of me?

This man welcomes sinners and eats with them. When have I felt unworthy of God's welcome? How does my sinfulness separate me from God and neighbor?

And when he does find it, he sets it on his shoulders with great joy. When have I felt God's loving support most strongly? When has my faith brought me joy?

There will be rejoicing among the angels of God over one sinner who repents. From what do I need to repent? What actions of mine give glory to God?

After a period of silent reflection and/or discussion, all recite the Lord's Prayer and the following:

Closing Prayer:

Have mercy on me, O God, in your goodness;
in the greatness of your compassion wipe out my offense.
Thoroughly wash me from my guilt
and of my sin cleanse me.

A clean heart create for me, O God,
and a steadfast spirit renew within me.
Cast me not out from your presence,
and your Holy Spirit take not from me.

O Lord, open my lips,
and my mouth shall proclaim your praise.
My sacrifice, O God, is a contrite spirit;
a heart contrite and humbled, O God, you will not spurn.

(From Psalm 51)

Living the Word This Week

How can I make my life a gift for others in charity?

Make a good examination of conscience and celebrate God's mercy in the Sacrament of Penance.

Thoughts for Today

September 22, 2019

Lectio Divina for the Twenty-Fifth Week in Ordinary Time

We begin our prayer:
In the name of the Father, and of the Son, and of the Holy Spirit. Amen.

O God, who founded all the commands of your sacred Law
upon love of you and of our neighbor,
grant that, by keeping your precepts,
we may merit to attain eternal life.
Through our Lord Jesus Christ, your Son,
who lives and reigns with you in the unity of the Holy Spirit,
one God, for ever and ever.

(Collect, Twenty-Fifth Sunday in Ordinary Time)

Reading (*Lectio*)

Read the following Scripture two or three times.
Luke 16:1-13

Jesus said to his disciples, "A rich man had a steward who was reported to him for squandering his property. He summoned him and said, 'What is this I hear about you? Prepare a full account of your stewardship, because you can no longer be my steward.' The steward said to himself, 'What shall I do, now that my master is taking the position of steward away from me? I am not strong enough to dig and I am ashamed to beg. I know what I shall do so that, when I am removed from the stewardship, they may welcome me into their homes.' He called in his master's debtors one by one. To the first he said, 'How much do you owe my master?' He replied, 'One hundred measures of olive oil.' He said to him, 'Here is your promissory note. Sit down and quickly write one for fifty.' Then to another the steward said, 'And you, how much do you owe?' He replied, 'One hundred kors of wheat.' The steward said to him, 'Here is your promissory note; write one for eighty.' And the master commended that dishonest steward for acting prudently.

"For the children of this world are more prudent in dealing with their own generation than are the children of light. I tell you, make friends for yourselves with dishonest wealth, so that when it fails, you will be welcomed into eternal dwellings. The person who is trustworthy in very small matters is also trustworthy in great ones; and the person who is dishonest in very small matters is also dishonest in great ones. If, therefore, you are not trustworthy with dishonest wealth, who will trust you with true wealth? If you are not trustworthy with what belongs to another, who will give you what is yours? No servant can serve two masters. He will either hate one and love the other, or be devoted to one and despise the other. You cannot serve both God and mammon."

Meditation (*Meditatio*)

After the reading, take some time to reflect in silence on one or more of the following questions:

- What word or words in this passage caught your attention?
- What in this passage comforted you?
- What in this passage challenged you?

If practicing lectio divina *as a family or in a group, after the reflection time, invite the participants to share their responses.*

Prayer (*Oratio*)

Read the Scripture passage one more time. Bring to the Lord the praise, petition, or thanksgiving that the Word inspires in you.

Contemplation (*Contemplatio*)

Read the Scripture again, followed by this reflection:

What conversion of mind, heart, and life is the Lord asking of me?

Prepare a full account of your stewardship, because you can no longer be my steward. How do I use the gifts God has given me? For what should I be grateful today?

The person who is dishonest in very small matters is also dishonest in great ones. When have I failed to live up to someone's trust? How can I make amends?

You cannot serve both God and mammon. How do I make sure that God is the priority in my life? What other things am I tempted to serve?

After a period of silent reflection and/or discussion, all recite the Lord's Prayer and the following:

Closing Prayer:

Praise, you servants of the LORD,
praise the name of the LORD.
Blessed be the name of the LORD
both now and forever.

High above all nations is the LORD;
above the heavens is his glory.
Who is like the LORD, our God, who is enthroned on high
and looks upon the heavens and the earth below?

He raises up the lowly from the dust;
from the dunghill he lifts up the poor
to seat them with princes,
with the princes of his own people.

(From Psalm 113)

Living the Word This Week

How can I make my life a gift for others in charity?

Learn more about authentic Christian stewardship:

http://www.usccb.org/beliefs-and-teachings/what-we-believe/stewardship/index.cfm.

Thoughts for Today

September 29, 2019

Lectio Divina for the Twenty-Sixth Week in Ordinary Time

We begin our prayer:
In the name of the Father, and of the Son, and of the Holy Spirit. Amen.

O God, who manifest your almighty power
above all by pardoning and showing mercy,
bestow, we pray, your grace abundantly upon us
and make those hastening to attain your promises
heirs to the treasures of heaven.
Through our Lord Jesus Christ, your Son,
who lives and reigns with you in the unity of the Holy Spirit,
one God, for ever and ever.

(Collect, Twenty-Sixth Sunday in Ordinary Time)

Reading (*Lectio*)

Read the following Scripture two or three times.
Luke 16:19-31

Jesus said to the Pharisees: "There was a rich man who dressed in purple garments and fine linen and dined sumptuously each day. And lying at his door was a poor man named Lazarus, covered with sores, who would gladly have eaten his fill of the scraps that fell from the rich man's table. Dogs even used to come and lick his sores. When the poor man died, he was carried away by angels to the bosom of Abraham. The rich man also died and was buried, and from the netherworld, where he was in torment, he raised his eyes and saw Abraham far off and Lazarus at his side. And he cried out, 'Father Abraham, have pity on me. Send Lazarus to dip the tip of his finger in water and cool my tongue, for I am suffering torment in these flames.' Abraham replied, 'My child, remember that you received what was good during your lifetime while Lazarus likewise received what was bad; but now he is comforted here, whereas you are tormented. Moreover, between us and you a great chasm is established to prevent anyone from crossing who might wish to go from our side to yours or from your side to ours.' He said, 'Then I beg you, father, send him to my father's house, for I have five brothers, so that he may warn them, lest they too come to this place of torment.' But Abraham replied, 'They have Moses and the prophets. Let them listen to them.' He said, 'Oh no, father Abraham, but if someone from the dead goes to them, they will repent.' Then Abraham said, 'If they will not listen to Moses and the prophets, neither will they be persuaded if someone should rise from the dead.'"

Meditation (*Meditatio*)

After the reading, take some time to reflect in silence on one or more of the following questions:

- What word or words in this passage caught your attention?
- What in this passage comforted you?
- What in this passage challenged you?

If practicing lectio divina *as a family or in a group, after the reflection time, invite the participants to share their responses.*

Prayer (*Oratio*)

Read the Scripture passage one more time. Bring to the Lord the praise, petition, or thanksgiving that the Word inspires in you.

Contemplation (*Contemplatio*)

Read the Scripture again, followed by this reflection:

What conversion of mind, heart, and life is the Lord asking of me?

And lying at his door was a poor man named Lazarus, covered with sores, who would gladly have eaten his fill of the scraps that fell from the rich man's table. When have I failed to recognize the needs of those around me? How can I be more attentive to those needs?

Moreover, between us and you a great chasm is established to prevent anyone from crossing who might wish to go from our side to yours or from your side to ours. What circumstances or attitudes create a chasm between me and those around me? How can I be a person who bridges that chasm?

If they will not listen to Moses and the prophets, neither will they be persuaded if someone should rise from the dead. When have I failed to listen to the teaching of the Church? How can I more effectively share the faith of the Church?

After a period of silent reflection and/or discussion, all recite the Lord's Prayer and the following:

Closing Prayer:

Blessed he who keeps faith forever,
secures justice for the oppressed,
gives food to the hungry.
The LORD sets captives free.

The LORD gives sight to the blind.
The LORD raises up those who were bowed down.
The LORD loves the just.
The LORD protects strangers.

The fatherless and the widow he sustains,
but the way of the wicked he thwarts.

The LORD shall reign forever;
your God, O Zion, through all generations.

(From Psalm 146)

Living the Word This Week

How can I make my life a gift for others in charity?

Participate in a parish, diocesan, or community service project to help those in need.

Thoughts for Today

October 6, 2019

Lectio Divina for the Twenty-Seventh Week in Ordinary Time

We begin our prayer:
In the name of the Father, and of the Son, and of the Holy Spirit.
Amen.

Almighty ever-living God,
who in the abundance of your kindness
surpass the merits and the desires of those who entreat you,
pour out your mercy upon us
to pardon what conscience dreads
and to give what prayer does not dare to ask.
Through our Lord Jesus Christ, your Son,
who lives and reigns with you in the unity of the Holy Spirit,
one God, for ever and ever.

(Collect, Twenty-Seventh Sunday in Ordinary Time)

Reading (*Lectio*)

Read the following Scripture two or three times.
Luke 17:5-10

The apostles said to the Lord, "Increase our faith." The Lord replied, "If you have faith the size of a mustard seed, you would say to this mulberry tree, 'Be uprooted and planted in the sea,' and it would obey you.

"Who among you would say to your servant who has just come in from plowing or tending sheep in the field, 'Come here immediately and take your place at table'? Would he not rather say to him, 'Prepare something for me to eat. Put on your apron and wait on me while I eat and drink. You may eat and drink when I am finished'? Is he grateful to that servant because he did what was commanded? So should it be with you. When you have done all you have been commanded, say, 'We are unprofitable servants; we have done what we were obliged to do.'"

Meditation (*Meditatio*)

After the reading, take some time to reflect in silence on one or more of the following questions:

- What word or words in this passage caught your attention?
- What in this passage comforted you?
- What in this passage challenged you?

If practicing lectio divina *as a family or in a group, after the reflection time, invite the participants to share their responses.*

Prayer (*Oratio*)

Read the Scripture passage one more time. Bring to the Lord the praise, petition, or thanksgiving that the Word inspires in you.

Contemplation (*Contemplatio*)

Read the Scripture again, followed by this reflection:

What conversion of mind, heart, and life is the Lord asking of me?

Increase our faith. What things challenge or undermine my faith? What makes my faith stronger?

Who among you would say to your servant who has just come in from plowing or tending sheep in the field, "Come here immediately and take your place at table"? How do I treat people in positions of service? How can I uphold the dignity of all people?

We are unprofitable servants; we have done what we were obliged to do. How can I serve God more faithfully? To what actions does my faith oblige me?

After a period of silent reflection and/or discussion, all recite the Lord's Prayer and the following:

Closing Prayer:

Come, let us sing joyfully to the LORD;
 let us acclaim the Rock of our salvation.
Let us come into his presence with thanksgiving;
 let us joyfully sing psalms to him.

Come, let us bow down in worship;
 let us kneel before the LORD who made us.
For he is our God,
 and we are the people he shepherds, the flock he guides.

Oh, that today you would hear his voice:
 "Harden not your hearts as at Meribah,
 as in the day of Massah in the desert,
Where your fathers tempted me;
 they tested me though they had seen my works."

(From Psalm 95)

Living the Word This Week

How can I make my life a gift for others in charity?

Commit to a weekly effort to learn more about your faith by taking a class, reading Catholic books or magazine, or listening to good Catholic programming on radio, television, or digital outlets.

Thoughts for Today

October 13, 2019

Lectio Divina for the Twenty-Eighth Week in Ordinary Time

We begin our prayer:
In the name of the Father, and of the Son, and of the Holy Spirit. Amen.

May your grace, O Lord, we pray,
at all times go before us and follow after
and make us always determined
to carry out good works.
Through our Lord Jesus Christ, your Son,
who lives and reigns with you in the unity of the Holy Spirit,
one God, for ever and ever.

(Collect, Twenty-Eighth Sunday in Ordinary Time)

Reading (*Lectio*)

Read the following Scripture two or three times.
Luke 17:11-19

As Jesus continued his journey to Jerusalem, he traveled through Samaria and Galilee. As he was entering a village, ten lepers met him. They stood at a distance from him and raised their voices, saying, "Jesus, Master! Have pity on us!" And when he saw them, he said, "Go show yourselves to the priests." As they were going they were cleansed. And one of them, realizing he had been healed, returned, glorifying God in a loud voice; and he fell at the feet of Jesus and thanked him. He was a Samaritan. Jesus said in reply, "Ten were cleansed, were they not? Where are the other nine? Has none but this foreigner returned to give thanks to God?" Then he said to him, "Stand up and go; your faith has saved you."

Meditation (*Meditatio*)

After the reading, take some time to reflect in silence on one or more of the following questions:

- What word or words in this passage caught your attention?
- What in this passage comforted you?
- What in this passage challenged you?

If practicing lectio divina *as a family or in a group, after the reflection time, invite the participants to share their responses.*

Prayer (*Oratio*)

Read the Scripture passage one more time. Bring to the Lord the praise, petition, or thanksgiving that the Word inspires in you.

Contemplation (*Contemplatio*)

Read the Scripture again, followed by this reflection:

What conversion of mind, heart, and life is the Lord asking of me?

They stood at a distance from him and raised their voices, saying, "Jesus, Master! Have pity on us!" What things distance me from Jesus? What parts of my life need to be touched by Jesus' pity?

Has none but this foreigner returned to give thanks to God? When have I failed to recognize the good things God has done for me? How can I demonstrate my gratitude to God in my daily life?

Stand up and go; your faith has saved you. Where am I being sent? How does my faith strengthen me for the journey?

After a period of silent reflection and/or discussion, all recite the Lord's Prayer and the following:

Closing Prayer:

Sing to the LORD a new song,
 for he has done wondrous deeds;
his right hand has won victory for him,
 his holy arm.

The LORD has made his salvation known:
 in the sight of the nations he has revealed his justice.
He has remembered his kindness and his faithfulness
 toward the house of Israel.

All the ends of the earth have seen
 the salvation by our God.
Sing joyfully to the LORD, all you lands:
 break into song; sing praise.

(From Psalm 98)

Living the Word This Week

How can I make my life a gift for others in charity?

"Eucharist" comes from the Greek word meaning "to give thanks." Make a list of the things for which you are grateful and give thanks for them during the Sunday liturgy.

Thoughts for Today

October 20, 2019

Lectio Divina for the Twenty-Ninth Week in Ordinary Time

We begin our prayer:
In the name of the Father, and of the Son, and of the Holy Spirit. Amen.

Almighty ever-living God,
grant that we may always conform our will to yours
and serve your majesty in sincerity of heart.
Through our Lord Jesus Christ, your Son,
who lives and reigns with you in the unity of the Holy Spirit,
one God, for ever and ever.

(Collect, Twenty-Ninth Sunday in Ordinary Time)

Reading (*Lectio*)

Read the following Scripture two or three times.
Luke 18:1-8

Jesus told his disciples a parable about the necessity for them to pray always without becoming weary. He said, "There was a judge in a certain town who neither feared God nor respected any human being. And a widow in that town used to come to him and say, 'Render a just decision for me against my adversary.' For a long time the judge was unwilling, but eventually he thought, 'While it is true that I neither fear God nor respect any human being, because this widow keeps bothering me I shall deliver a just decision for her lest she finally come and strike me.'" The Lord said, "Pay attention to what the dishonest judge says. Will not God then secure the rights of his chosen ones who call out to him day and night? Will he be slow to answer them? I tell you, he will see to it that justice is done for them speedily. But when the Son of Man comes, will he find faith on earth?"

Meditation (*Meditatio*)

After the reading, take some time to reflect in silence on one or more of the following questions:

- What word or words in this passage caught your attention?
- What in this passage comforted you?
- What in this passage challenged you?

If practicing lectio divina *as a family or in a group, after the reflection time, invite the participants to share their responses.*

Prayer (*Oratio*)

Read the Scripture passage one more time. Bring to the Lord the praise, petition, or thanksgiving that the Word inspires in you.

Contemplation (*Contemplatio*)

Read the Scripture again, followed by this reflection:

What conversion of mind, heart, and life is the Lord asking of me?

Jesus told his disciples a parable about the necessity for them to pray always without becoming weary. What causes me to get tired of praying? How can I deal with the times when God seems silent?

He will see to it that justice is done for them speedily. What can I do to make the world more just? How does God's justice differ from the common understanding of justice?

But when the Son of Man comes, will he find faith on earth? How can I prepare my heart for Jesus' second coming? How do I put my faith into practice?

After a period of silent reflection and/or discussion, all recite the Lord's Prayer and the following:

Closing Prayer:

I lift up my eyes toward the mountains;
  whence shall help come to me?
My help is from the LORD,
  who made heaven and earth.

May he not suffer your foot to slip;
  may he slumber not who guards you:
indeed he neither slumbers nor sleeps,
  the guardian of Israel.

The LORD is your guardian; the LORD is your shade;
  he is beside you at your right hand.
The sun shall not harm you by day,
  nor the moon by night.

The LORD will guard you from all evil;
  he will guard your life.
The LORD will guard your coming and your going,
  both now and forever.

(From Psalm 121)

Living the Word This Week

How can I make my life a gift for others in charity?

Learn more about restorative justice here:

http://www.usccb.org/issues-and-action/human-life-and-dignity/criminal-justice-restorative-justice/crime-and-criminal-justice.cfm.

Thoughts for Today

October 27, 2019

Lectio Divina for the Thirtieth Week in Ordinary Time

We begin our prayer:
In the name of the Father, and of the Son, and of the Holy Spirit. Amen.

Almighty ever-living God,
increase our faith, hope and charity,
and make us love what you command,
so that we may merit what you promise.
Through our Lord Jesus Christ, your Son,
who lives and reigns with you in the unity of the Holy Spirit,
one God, for ever and ever.

(Collect, Thirtieth Sunday in Ordinary Time)

Reading (*Lectio*)

Read the following Scripture two or three times.
Luke 18:9-14

Jesus addressed this parable to those who were convinced of their own righteousness and despised everyone else. "Two people went up to the temple area to pray; one was a Pharisee and the other was a tax collector. The Pharisee took up his position and spoke this prayer to himself, 'O God, I thank you that I am not like the rest of humanity—greedy, dishonest, adulterous—or even like this tax collector. I fast twice a week, and I pay tithes on my whole income.' But the tax collector stood off at a distance and would not even raise his eyes to heaven but beat his breast and prayed, 'O God, be merciful to me a sinner.' I tell you, the latter went home justified, not the former; for whoever exalts himself will be humbled, and the one who humbles himself will be exalted."

Meditation (*Meditatio*)

After the reading, take some time to reflect in silence on one or more of the following questions:

- What word or words in this passage caught your attention?
- What in this passage comforted you?
- What in this passage challenged you?

If practicing lectio divina *as a family or in a group, after the reflection time, invite the participants to share their responses.*

Prayer (*Oratio*)

Read the Scripture passage one more time. Bring to the Lord the praise, petition, or thanksgiving that the Word inspires in you.

Contemplation (*Contemplatio*)

Read the Scripture again, followed by this reflection:

What conversion of mind, heart, and life is the Lord asking of me?

Jesus addressed this parable to those who were convinced of their own righteousness and despised everyone else. How often do I judge my spiritual progress against other people's? What prejudices or biases do I need to purge from my heart?

I fast twice a week, and I pay tithes on my whole income. How can I deepen the devotion of my religious practice? What religious practices draw me closer to God?

But the tax collector stood off at a distance and would not even raise his eyes to heaven but beat his breast and prayed, "O God, be merciful to me a sinner." How can I be more attentive to my own sinfulness and need for God's mercy? How can I share God's message of love and forgiveness?

After a period of silent reflection and/or discussion, all recite te Lord's Prayer and the following:

Closing Prayer:

I will bless the LORD at all times;
 his praise shall be ever in my mouth.
Let my soul glory in the LORD;
 the lowly will hear me and be glad.

The LORD confronts the evildoers,
 to destroy remembrance of them from the earth.
When the just cry out, the LORD hears them,
 and from all their distress he rescues them.

The LORD is close to the brokenhearted;
 and those who are crushed in spirit he saves.
The LORD redeems the lives of his servants;
 no one incurs guilt who takes refuge in him.

(From Psalm 34)

Living the Word This Week

How can I make my life a gift for others in charity?

Pray the "Jesus Prayer" ("O God, be merciful to me a sinner.") for five minutes each day.

Thoughts for Today

November 1, 2019

Lectio Divina for the Solemnity of All Saints

We begin our prayer:
In the name of the Father, and of the Son, and of the Holy Spirit.
Amen.

Almighty ever-living God,
by whose gift we venerate in one celebration
the merits of all the Saints,
bestow on us, we pray,
through the prayers of so many intercessors,
an abundance of the reconciliation with you
for which we earnestly long.
Through our Lord Jesus Christ, your Son,
who lives and reigns with you in the unity of the Holy Spirit,
one God, for ever and ever.

(Collect, Solemnity of All Saints)

Reading (*Lectio*)

Read the following Scripture two or three times.
Matthew 5:1-12a

When Jesus saw the crowds, he went up the mountain, and after he had sat down, his disciples came to him. He began to teach them, saying:

> "Blessed are the poor in spirit,
> for theirs is the Kingdom of heaven.
> Blessed are they who mourn,
> for they will be comforted.

Blessed are the meek,
for they will inherit the land.
Blessed are they who hunger and thirst for righteousness,
for they will be satisfied.
Blessed are the merciful,
for they will be shown mercy.
Blessed are the clean of heart,
for they will see God.
Blessed are the peacemakers,
for they will be called children of God.
Blessed are they who are persecuted for the sake of righteousness,
for theirs is the Kingdom of heaven.
Blessed are you when they insult you and persecute you
and utter every kind of evil against you falsely because of me.
Rejoice and be glad, for your reward will be great in heaven."

Meditation (*Meditatio*)

After the reading, take some time to reflect in silence on one or more of the following questions:

- What word or words in this passage caught your attention?
- What in this passage comforted you?
- What in this passage challenged you?

If practicing lectio divina *as a family or in a group, after the reflection time, invite the participants to share their responses.*

Prayer (*Oratio*)

Read the Scripture passage one more time. Bring to the Lord the praise, petition, or thanksgiving that the Word inspires in you.

Contemplation (*Contemplatio*)

Read the Scripture again, followed by this reflection:

What conversion of mind, heart, and life is the Lord asking of me?

Blessed are they who hunger and thirst for righteousness, / for they will be satisfied. For what does my soul hunger? How can I feed my soul?

Blessed are the merciful, / for they will be shown mercy. Who do I need to forgive? What grudges do I need to release?

Blessed are the clean of heart, / for they will see God. What fears, anxieties, and preoccupations cloud my heart? How can I become more attentive to God's presence in my life?

After a period of silent reflection and/or discussion, all recite the Lord's Prayer and the following:

Closing Prayer:

The LORD's are the earth and its fullness;
the world and those who dwell in it.
For he founded it upon the seas
and established it upon the rivers.

Who can ascend the mountain of the LORD?
or who may stand in his holy place?
One whose hands are sinless, whose heart is clean,
who desires not what is vain.

He shall receive a blessing from the LORD,
a reward from God his savior.
Such is the race that seeks him,
that seeks the face of the God of Jacob.

(From Psalm 24)

Living the Word This Week

How can I make my life a gift for others in charity?

Read Pope Francis's Apostolic Exhortation, *Rejoice and Be Glad*:

http://w2.vatican.va/content/francesco/en/apost_exhortations/documents/papa-francesco_esortazione-ap_20180319_gaudete-et-exsultate.html.

Thoughts for Today

November 3, 2019

Lectio Divina for the Thirty-First Week in Ordinary Time

We begin our prayer:
In the name of the Father, and of the Son, and of the Holy Spirit.
Amen.

Almighty and merciful God,
by whose gift your faithful offer you
right and praiseworthy service,
grant, we pray,
that we may hasten without stumbling
to receive the things you have promised.
Through our Lord Jesus Christ, your Son,
who lives and reigns with you in the unity of the Holy Spirit,
one God, for ever and ever.

(Collect, Thirty-First Sunday in Ordinary Time)

Reading (*Lectio*)

Read the following Scripture two or three times.
Luke 19:1-10

At that time, Jesus came to Jericho and intended to pass through the town. Now a man there named Zacchaeus, who was a chief tax collector and also a wealthy man, was seeking to see who Jesus was; but he could not see him because of the crowd, for he was short in stature. So he ran ahead and climbed a sycamore tree in order to see Jesus, who was about to pass that way. When he reached the place, Jesus looked up and said, "Zacchaeus, come down quickly, for today

I must stay at your house." And he came down quickly and received him with joy. When they all saw this, they began to grumble, saying, "He has gone to stay at the house of a sinner." But Zacchaeus stood there and said to the Lord, "Behold, half of my possessions, Lord, I shall give to the poor, and if I have extorted anything from anyone I shall repay it four times over." And Jesus said to him, "Today salvation has come to this house because this man too is a descendant of Abraham. For the Son of Man has come to seek and to save what was lost."

Meditation (*Meditatio*)

After the reading, take some time to reflect in silence on one or more of the following questions:

- What word or words in this passage caught your attention?
- What in this passage comforted you?
- What in this passage challenged you?

If practicing lectio divina *as a family or in a group, after the reflection time, invite the participants to share their responses.*

Prayer (*Oratio*)

Read the Scripture passage one more time. Bring to the Lord the praise, petition, or thanksgiving that the Word inspires in you.

Contemplation (*Contemplatio*)

Read the Scripture again, followed by this reflection:

What conversion of mind, heart, and life is the Lord asking of me?

Now a man there named Zacchaeus, who was a chief tax collector and also a wealthy man, was seeking to see who Jesus was; but he could not see him because of the crowd, for he was short in stature. What prevents me from seeing Jesus? How do my actions help or prevent others from seeing Jesus?

And he came down quickly and received him with joy. When was the last time I answered God's call with joy? What obstacles keep me from obeying God's will?

For the Son of Man has come to seek and to save what was lost. When have I felt lost? How is my faith a beacon to me in those times?

After a period of silent reflection and/or discussion, all recite the Lord's Prayer and the following:

Closing Prayer:

I will extol you, O my God and King,
    and I will bless your name forever and ever.
Every day will I bless you,
    and I will praise your name forever and ever.

The LORD is gracious and merciful,
    slow to anger and of great kindness.
The LORD is good to all
    and compassionate toward all his works.

Let all your works give you thanks, O LORD,
    and let your faithful ones bless you.
Let them discourse of the glory of your kingdom
    and speak of your might.

The LORD is faithful in all his words
    and holy in all his works.
The LORD lifts up all who are falling
    and raises up all who are bowed down.

(From Psalm 145)

Living the Word This Week

How can I make my life a gift for others in charity?

Invite someone to attend Mass or another church event with you.

Thoughts for Today

November 10, 2019

Lectio Divina for the Thirty-Second Week in Ordinary Time

We begin our prayer:
In the name of the Father, and of the Son, and of the Holy Spirit. Amen.

Almighty and merciful God,
graciously keep from us all adversity,
so that, unhindered in mind and body alike,
we may pursue in freedom of heart
the things that are yours.
Through our Lord Jesus Christ, your Son,
who lives and reigns with you in the unity of the Holy Spirit,
one God, for ever and ever.

(Collect, Thirty-Second Sunday in Ordinary Time)

Reading (*Lectio*)

Read the following Scripture two or three times.
Luke 20:27-38

Some Sadducees, those who deny that there is a resurrection, came forward and put this question to Jesus, saying, "Teacher, Moses wrote for us, *If someone's brother dies leaving a wife but no child, his brother must take the wife and raise up descendants for his brother.* Now there were seven brothers; the first married a woman but died childless. Then the second and the third married her, and likewise all the seven died childless. Finally the woman also died. Now at the resurrection whose wife will that woman be? For all seven had been married to her." Jesus said to them, "The children of this age marry and remarry; but those who are deemed worthy to attain to the coming age and to the resurrection of the dead neither marry nor are given in marriage. They can no longer die, for they are like angels; and they are the children of God because they are the ones who will rise. That the dead will rise even Moses made known in the passage about the bush, when he called out 'Lord,' the God of Abraham, the God of Isaac, and the God of Jacob; and he is not God of the dead, but of the living, for to him all are alive."

Meditation (*Meditatio*)

After the reading, take some time to reflect in silence on one or more of the following questions:

- What word or words in this passage caught your attention?
- What in this passage comforted you?
- What in this passage challenged you?

If practicing lectio divina *as a family or in a group, after the reflection time, invite the participants to share their responses.*

Prayer (*Oratio*)

Read the Scripture passage one more time. Bring to the Lord the praise, petition, or thanksgiving that the Word inspires in you.

Contemplation (*Contemplatio*)

Read the Scripture again, followed by this reflection:

What conversion of mind, heart, and life is the Lord asking of me?

Some Sadducees, those who deny that there is a resurrection, came forward and put this question to Jesus. How do I deal with those who deny important aspects of my faith? How do I respond to questions about my faith?

They are the children of God because they are the ones who will rise. How does my belief in the resurrection affect my daily life? How does seeing people as children of God change my views and behavior?

He is not God of the dead, but of the living, for to him all are alive. What practices or devotions give new life to my faith? How does my faith unite me to love ones who have died?

After a period of silent reflection and/or discussion, all recite the Lord's Prayer and the following:

Closing Prayer:

Hear, O LORD, a just suit;
attend to my outcry;
hearken to my prayer from lips without deceit.

My steps have been steadfast in your paths,
my feet have not faltered.
I call upon you, for you will answer me, O God;
incline your ear to me; hear my word.

Keep me as the apple of your eye,
hide me in the shadow of your wings.
But I in justice shall behold your face;
on waking I shall be content in your presence.

(From Psalm 17)

Living the Word This Week

How can I make my life a gift for others in charity?

Volunteer with your parish bereavement ministry or visit a Catholic cemetery. Pray for those who have died who have no one to pray for them.

Thoughts for Today

November 17, 2019

Lectio Divina for the Thirty-Third Week in Ordinary Time

We begin our prayer:
In the name of the Father, and of the Son, and of the Holy Spirit. Amen.

Grant us, we pray, O Lord our God,
the constant gladness of being devoted to you,
for it is full and lasting happiness
to serve with constancy
the author of all that is good.
Through our Lord Jesus Christ, your Son,
who lives and reigns with you in the unity of the Holy Spirit,
one God, for ever and ever.

(Collect, Thirty-Third Sunday in Ordinary Time)

Reading (*Lectio*)

Read the following Scripture two or three times.
Luke 21:5-19

While some people were speaking about how the temple was adorned with costly stones and votive offerings, Jesus said, "All that you see here—the days will come when there will not be left a stone upon another stone that will not be thrown down."

Then they asked him, "Teacher, when will this happen? And what sign will there be when all these things are about to happen?" He answered, "See that you not be deceived, for many will come in my name, saying, 'I am he,' and 'The time has come.' Do not follow them! When you hear of wars and insurrections, do not be terrified;

for such things must happen first, but it will not immediately be the end." Then he said to them, "Nation will rise against nation, and kingdom against kingdom. There will be powerful earthquakes, famines, and plagues from place to place; and awesome sights and mighty signs will come from the sky.

"Before all this happens, however, they will seize and persecute you, they will hand you over to the synagogues and to prisons, and they will have you led before kings and governors because of my name. It will lead to your giving testimony. Remember, you are not to prepare your defense beforehand, for I myself shall give you a wisdom in speaking that all your adversaries will be powerless to resist or refute. You will even be handed over by parents, brothers, relatives, and friends, and they will put some of you to death. You will be hated by all because of my name, but not a hair on your head will be destroyed. By your perseverance you will secure your lives."

Meditation (*Meditatio*)

After the reading, take some time to reflect in silence on one or more of the following questions:

- What word or words in this passage caught your attention?
- What in this passage comforted you?
- What in this passage challenged you?

If practicing lectio divina *as a family or in a group, after the reflection time, invite the participants to share their responses.*

Prayer (*Oratio*)

Read the Scripture passage one more time. Bring to the Lord the praise, petition, or thanksgiving that the Word inspires in you.

Contemplation (*Contemplatio*)

Read the Scripture again, followed by this reflection:

What conversion of mind, heart, and life is the Lord asking of me?

Many will come in my name, saying, "I am he," and "The time has come." Do not follow them! What false paths am I tempted to follow? How do I discern the path to which God is calling me?

You will be hated by all because of my name. When have I suffered ridicule or teasing because of my faith? When have I shown bias toward others because of their faith?

By your perseverance you will secure your lives. When do I struggle to remain faithful? What supports my faith in difficult times?

After a period of silent reflection and/or discussion, all recite the Lord's Prayer and the following:

Closing Prayer:

Sing praise to the LORD with the harp,
with the harp and melodious song.
With trumpets and the sound of the horn
sing joyfully before the King, the LORD.

Let the sea and what fills it resound,
the world and those who dwell in it;
let the rivers clap their hands,
the mountains shout with them for joy.

Before the LORD, for he comes,
for he comes to rule the earth,
He will rule the world with justice
and the peoples with equity.

(From Psalm 98)

Living the Word This Week

How can I make my life a gift for others in charity?

Learn more about Church teaching on religious liberty:

http://www.usccb.org/issues-and-action/religious-liberty/church-teaching-on-religious-liberty.cfm.

Thoughts for Today

November 24, 2019

Lectio Divina for the Solemnity of Jesus Christ, King of the Universe

We begin our prayer:
In the name of the Father, and of the Son, and of the Holy Spirit. Amen.

Almighty ever-living God,
whose will is to restore all things
in your beloved Son, the King of the universe,
grant, we pray,
that the whole creation, set free from slavery,
may render your majesty service
and ceaselessly proclaim your praise.
Through our Lord Jesus Christ, your Son,
who lives and reigns with you in the unity of the Holy Spirit,
one God, for ever and ever.

(Collect, Christ the King)

Reading (*Lectio*)

Read the following Scripture two or three times.
Luke 23:35-43

The rulers sneered at Jesus and said, "He saved others, let him save himself if he is the chosen one, the Christ of God." Even the soldiers jeered at him. As they approached to offer him wine they called out, "If you are King of the Jews, save yourself." Above him there was an inscription that read, "This is the King of the Jews."

Now one of the criminals hanging there reviled Jesus, saying, "Are you not the Christ? Save yourself and us." The other, however, rebuking him, said in reply, "Have you no fear of God, for you are subject to the same condemnation? And indeed, we have been condemned justly, for the sentence we received corresponds to our crimes, but this man has done nothing criminal." Then he said, "Jesus, remember me when you come into your kingdom." He replied to him, "Amen, I say to you, today you will be with me in Paradise."

Meditation (*Meditatio*)

After the reading, take some time to reflect in silence on one or more of the following questions:

- What word or words in this passage caught your attention?
- What in this passage comforted you?
- What in this passage challenged you?

If practicing lectio divina *as a family or in a group, after the reflection time, invite the participants to share their responses.*

Prayer (*Oratio*)

Read the Scripture passage one more time. Bring to the Lord the praise, petition, or thanksgiving that the Word inspires in you.

Contemplation (*Contemplatio*)

Read the Scripture again, followed by this reflection:

What conversion of mind, heart, and life is the Lord asking of me?

Are you not the Christ? Save yourself and us. When have I questioned Christ? How can I best address those times when my faith feels weakest?

Have you no fear of God? When do I feel awe for God and his works? How can I become more aware of God's majesty and power working in my life?

Jesus, remember me when you come into your kingdom. When

have I felt forgotten? What reminds me of God's presence and love for me?

After a period of silent reflection and/or discussion, all recite the Lord's Prayer and the following:

Closing Prayer:

I rejoiced because they said to me,
  "We will go up to the house of the LORD."
And now we have set foot
  within your gates, O Jerusalem.

Jerusalem, built as a city
  with compact unity.
To it the tribes go up,
  the tribes of the LORD.

According to the decree for Israel,
  to give thanks to the name of the LORD.
In it are set up judgment seats,
  seats for the house of David.

(From Psalm 122)

Living the Word This Week

How can I make my life a gift for others in charity?

Remember those who have asked for your prayers.

Thoughts for Today